HOPE CHEST

HOPE CHEST

A Treasure of
Spiritual Keepsakes

ROD TERRY

Enaas Publishing
Washington, DC

Enaas Publishing
18 R Street, NW
Washington, DC 20001

ISBN 978-0-9814586-5-6
Library of Congress Number: 2008900445
First edition
Printed and bound in the United States of America

Cover Artwork: Donna Boozer
Cover and Interior Design: SUN Editing & Book Design
(suneditwrite.com)

Excerpt from *Choose To Be Happy* by Swami Chetanananda ©1996.
Reprinted by permission of Rudra Press.

Library of Congress Cataloging-in-Publication Data

Terry, Rod.
    Hope chest : a treasure of spiritual keepsakes / Rod Terry.
    p. cm.
    ISBN 978-0-9814586-5-6

1. Conduct of life. 2. Inspiration. 3. Self-help techniques--Anecdotes.
4. Self-perception. 5. Self-evaluation. I. Title.

BJ1597 .T48 2008
170.4421--dc22   2008900445

To my grandmother, Corine Parks,

to whom I am devoted

Contents

*The growing edge of hope remains
when all the voices of despair are stilled.*

— Howard Thurman

*Out of the lowest depths
there is a path to the loftiest height.*

— Thomas Carlyle

Introduction

Years ago, while helping my grandmother clean her attic, I stumbled upon a wooden box buried in the corner. My grandmother told me it was a family keepsake that had been given to her by her mother, my great-grandmother. Observing my interest in the box, she told me the story of how generations ago it was tradition for mothers to purchase trunks or large wooden boxes for their daughters. The trunks were used to collect and store linen, silver, china and other household articles for safekeeping until the daughter married or left home. Those trunks or boxes were called "hope chests."

My grandmother's hope chest was beautiful. It was an ornate cherry wood box with intricate carvings and other adornments. It measured about eighteen inches wide, forty inches long and two feet deep. Surprisingly, it was in good condition. Even the brass latch gleamed when the sunlight from the window hit it. According to my grandmother, when she received her hope chest more than fifty years ago, it contained a Bible, two silver candelabras, a patchwork quilt, a porcelain angel, a hand-held mirror and a washboard.

Anxious to know what remained in the chest, I opened it. Unfortunately, it contained only remnants of old documents and other knickknacks that had been placed there and forgotten, much like the chest itself. Yet, I could imagine the love and care that my great-grandmother had dispensed in preparing the hope chest for my grandmother's journey into womanhood. I sensed from my grandmother's facial expression that her hope chest was still a source of great pride and fond memories.

For my grandmother, the hope chest represented the future. It gave her the security of knowing that she could make the transition from childhood to womanhood with some of the essentials necessary to build a new life. It also provided her a foundation steeped in pride and tradition — a tradition she would pass to her children.

The beauty and historical legacy of the hope chest fascinated me. I was impressed with the meticulous planning and calculated efforts that had been made to prepare a child to leave the familiar nest of home. I envisioned my great-grandmother placing a special item into her daughter's hope chest each year of my grandmother's life, necessities she believed would assist my grandmother's ability to build a home and instill hope for the future.

After hearing the story of the tradition from my grandmother, it occurred to me that each of us needs our own "hope chest" of comforting and inspiring words to draw from as we journey through life. Like the original tradition, it would provide promises of hope and inspiration for the future.

Today is a challenging time to live in the world. Many of us are searching for meaning and purpose in our lives. To help fill the empty space, I have created a figurative "hope chest" in the pages that follow. *Hope Chest* contains a treasure of spiritual keepsakes and inspirational stories to renew the spirit and refresh the soul.

At the conclusion of each passage in the book, there is also a special *Keepsake* designed to reinforce the message in the passage. The *Keepsakes* are affirmations, or positive statements, that you can memorize and repeat throughout the day. *Keepsakes* are an important part of the book, because they empower you to become your own source of power and strength.

Hope Chest is, in short, a spiritual survival kit designed to ease the discomforts of life and to help you get through the rough times with your heart and soul intact. It is my prayer that *Hope Chest* will provide insight, spiritual guidance and inspiration for dealing with the daily challenges of life.

PART ONE

Private Pilgrimages

~

Life is an inward journey.
Every day we must go within and
find our inner strength.

Practice Self-Love

Love takes off masks that we fear we cannot live without and know we cannot live within.

— James Baldwin

There is no greater love than the love for oneself. Our first order of business each day should be to greet ourselves with admiration and love. Can you look in the mirror and say without reservation that you are in love with the person you see? For many of us, this is a difficult question, because we do not see ourselves as the object of love. Our self-image is often fragmented because of a sense of inadequacy or unworthiness. We love deeply when it comes to our parents, spouses, children and friends, but we do not always view ourselves in the same endearing way. Rather than embrace ourselves, we tend to search for outside sources of love and affirmation. Ironically, we expect the world to love and accept us, even when we do not love and accept ourselves.

I know firsthand that self-love and self-affirmation can be a challenge. Throughout my life, loving myself in a meaningful way has been an area of continuous struggle. Having grown up in a single-parent home with a speech impediment, I felt that I was not good enough, or I did not measure up to the other children in my neighborhood. In my small town, everything depended on where you lived, your parents' occupations and the type of car they drove. Against such a backdrop of superficiality and my own sense of inadequacy, it was difficult for me to love myself or see the value of my life. My insecurities were compounded by my parents' divorce when I was nine years old, which deepened the emotional void.

Compensating for my perceived shortcomings, I created a false self-image to conceal my lack of self-worth and shield myself from negative judgments. By reading magazines, watching television and observing others, I learned to dress, speak and conduct myself in a manner that I thought would make me fit in with the crowd. At that point in my life, I had no control over where I lived or my parents' income, but I could personally control how I presented myself to the world.

Of course, I created my identity at the expense of who I really was and how I really felt. Even so, I was resolute in my deception. My façade was so thick that all the king's horses and all the king's men could not pull it away. I was determined not to reveal my true self.

Naturally, my self-deception continued into my adult life. The older I grew, the more time I spent perfecting and refining my exterior image — expensive clothes, advanced degrees, luxury cars — whatever it took to make the right impression. I allowed how I looked on the outside to dictate how I felt inside.

Eventually, after many years of silent suffering, empty feelings, failed relationships and introspection, I realized that I needed to get beyond my external self-image and focus on inner awareness. I had grown tired of crashing into wall after wall, and began to search for ways to transform my life. Only through a long journey of forgiveness and acceptance was I able to see myself in a more authentic, loving way.

Most of us will go to great lengths to win the admiration and approval of others, but will do little to cultivate our own inner landscape. An important aspect of our journey toward a richer and more meaningful life is to recognize that our greatest reservoir of love is found within. It is not necessary to create a flawless exterior, seek the approval of others or cling to another person in search of love. Love is an *inside* job. No one else can love us more.

Practicing self-love means that we accept ourselves completely as we are — kinky hair, full lips, dysfunctional family, crooked teeth, love handles — and recognize that the source of our beauty is internal. Self-love is the starting point from which everything else in life flows. When we love, accept and respect ourselves, we become intimately aware of our worth, as well as the worth of others. We are able to share the infinite love that sustains us all and gives us our reason for being.

The ability to love and see the beauty in ourselves allows us to overcome feelings of inadequacy and un-worthiness. Self-love emboldens us with a greater sense of who we are. It gives us the confidence to be ourselves without seeking validation. It prevents us from becoming entangled in dependent and destructive relationships, second-guessing ourselves or succumbing to the desires and expectations of others. It also makes it possible for us to live on our own terms, without judging others or ourselves.

Although the importance and benefits of self-love are clear, learning to love ourselves is not an easy process; instead, it is a lifetime commitment that requires continuous nurturing. Like marriage vows, we must promise to love, cherish and accept every aspect of our-selves, for better or for worse, through good times and bad. We should apply the same level of love and devo-tion that we give our significant others to ourselves. The writer Oscar Wilde proclaimed, "To love oneself is the beginning of a life-long romance."

By loving ourselves truly and deeply, we expand our ability to love others. Self-love allows us to transcend personal needs and limitations and embrace those around us more readily. It also inspires a greater happiness and appreciation for life. When we are the center of our own affection, everyone and everything that comes on our path is influenced by our self-love.

Sometimes we are reluctant to practice self-love in a meaningful way because we fear others will view us as self-absorbed or conceited. However, genuine self-love transcends narcissism or arrogance. Self-love and trust in who we are, is what gives us the courage to be ourselves.

Keepsake

Do not go searching for love. The love you desire is already within you. To be loved or to love someone else, you have to love yourself first. The more you love yourself, the more love you can extend to others.

A Higher Purpose

Our presence on earth has intended consequences. There is a calling in each of our lives. We are on earth for a particular purpose, a divine mission. Our responsibility is to discover our purpose and faithfully pursue it. Whether we are called to promote peace, pursue justice, build bridges, educate children, plant trees or mold pottery, every moment of our lives should be spent living with purpose.

One of the most tragic consequences in life results from living day-to-day without a sense of purpose. A sense of purpose is essential. It provides a road map that guides and directs our journey. Living purposefully makes life worth living. It gives us a reason to get up in the morning and face a new day. When we live with purpose, we feel that our actions are aligned with the will of God. Each step we take is divinely inspired.

My neighbor, who is a photographer, walks in such manner. His work seems to be motivated by a higher

12

force. He lives and breathes his craft. Rarely does one see him without his camera strapped over his shoulder, waiting to document the unfolding of life. Every photograph he takes magically captures the essence and soul of his subject. Given the vitality and depth of his work, it is clear that taking pictures is a natural extension of his life. It is a blessing to be able to do what we are put here to do.

When we recognize our purpose and live accordingly, our paradigm of how we view ourselves and the world shifts to a higher level. We are able to approach life with genuine interest and spiritual focus. Without a sense of purpose to guide us, our lives can drift in any direction. Any temptation can influence or distract us.

Purpose is our deepest spiritual dimension. There is no greater calling in life than self-love and fulfillment. Purpose defines the core of our existence. How do we discover our purpose? Our calling in life rarely reveals itself to us without serious introspection and self-evaluation. Living purposefully is a process of searching deep within our hearts and souls. To uncover our purpose, we must ask ourselves difficult yet fundamental questions: *Who am I? What is the meaning of my life? What is my heart's desire?* Answering these questions requires more than philosophical pondering. It provides an opportunity to examine our true essence and explore our most hidden desires. Although visible and tangible answers may not appear immediately, we must never stop asking questions of ourselves. It is only through this type of self-inquiry and contemplation that we can discover our true purpose.

No one else can hear our calling. We are the arbiters of our own destiny. Although our parents, family and friends have good intentions, we cannot adopt their expectations as our purpose; following the desires of others breeds conformity. Each of us must do the inner work to discover his or her purpose. We must listen to our inner voice, trust the guidance of our intuition and follow the passion of our heart. At the end of our journey, our greatest gift to humanity and ourselves is the feeling that our life mattered and that we made a difference in the world.

Keepsake

You were born with a purpose. Each day, resolve to discover your calling, so you can share your special gifts with the world.

Think Positively

Let your thoughts be positive for they will become your words. Let your words be positive for they will become your actions. Let your actions be positive for they will become your values. Let your values be positive for they will become your destiny.

— Mahatma Gandhi

Our lives are shaped by the contours of our thoughts. How we think reflects who we are. None of our thoughts is neutral or insignificant — they all produce consequences. Every thought that crosses our minds sends a message to the nerves, cells and muscles of the body, which generates an active response. We attract people, things and circumstances that correspond with our thoughts. For example, negative, acerbic thoughts create feelings of insecurity and defeat. They are like a ball and chain. They hold us back and prevent us from reaching our full potential. Loving, positive thoughts, on the other hand, attract prosperity and good fortune. They create a feeling that nothing can prevent us from achieving success and reaching our goals.

Our thoughts can be our most valuable asset. They have the power to make us or break us. By shifting our minds, we can transform ourselves from a position of weakness to a position of strength, from a state of despair to a state of happiness. We have the mental capacity to create any experience we desire. Whether we fuel our minds with negative or positive energy is a matter of choice.

Some years ago, I attended a local beauty pageant in my hometown. Of the eleven young women who participated in the pageant, the two front-runners were exceptionally poised and talented. Competition between them was stiff. During the talent performances, the first woman sang a soul-stirring medley of Lena Horne songs, which brought the audience to its feet. The other woman sang an equally moving rendition of the *Porgy and Bess* classic, "Summertime." Both performances received loud applause from the audience and high scores from the judges. It became apparent to everyone present that the victory would go to the woman who performed better in the question-and-answer segment of the pageant.

During the question competition, the contestant who was not answering was sequestered backstage. The master of ceremonies asked each participant the same question: "*What do you feel is your greatest asset?*" The first woman hedged, but then responded, "That's a very difficult question for me to answer. There are many areas in my life I would like to improve. I believe I am a wonderful and loving person, but I also have many shortcomings." The applause was respectful. Before answering the same question, her challenger hesitated for a moment, then held her head high and stated, "I am the epitome of womanhood. I am intelligent. I am beautiful. And I have the potential to do anything I choose!" The audience gave her a standing ovation. Needless to say, she won the pageant. This story demonstrates the value of positive thinking. When we fill our minds with positive thoughts about ourselves and others, our possibilities increase exponentially.

The key to personal transformation is being able to see the positive in every situation. Being positive means that rather than complaining about a situation, we learn from it. Being positive means that we accept others as they are instead of finding fault in them or passing judgment on them. Being positive means taking risks and embracing the unfamiliar. Being positive means being able to view ourselves in the most favorable light. Try to adopt this mindset as part of your everyday experience and see how your life changes.

According to experts, the mind cannot process two competing thoughts at the same time. By filling our minds with positive thoughts of love, courage, success, understanding, compassion, enthusiasm and happiness, we decrease our chance of being influenced by negative and destructive thinking. One way to do this is through a mental process called "pivoting." With the precision of a color guard, pivoting allows us to shift quickly from a negative thought to a thought that evokes happier emotions. For example, I am entertaining negative thoughts about a slight I received from my co-worker a month ago. I realize that I need to introduce a better feeling right now. In order to pivot from this negative thought to a more positive mindset, I imagine that I am on a tropical island in Jamaica watching the sunset. Immediately, I feel better and open channels for other positive thoughts to enter. Pivoting works every time. It is a good habit to keep a storehouse of positive thoughts, affirmations or mental pictures that enable us to pivot at the moment our minds drift toward negative thinking. Negative thoughts drain our energy and undermine our potential for self-love. By contrast, positive thoughts lift our spirits and make it possible for us to become our truest selves.

Keepsake

Who you think you are is who you will become. Life moves in the direction of your most dominant thoughts. Positive thoughts create positive circumstances.

Define Success for Yourself

A common denominator in human experience is our desire for a successful life. Whether a young woman from Nantucket, an old man from Harlem, an immigrant from Cuba or an orphan from Malawi, each has a burning desire to succeed. Success has many faces, but we all want to feel that our lives matter and that we make a difference. Achieving personal success is the crowning glory of life. It is the culmination of all our hopes, dreams and aspirations.

Success is available for each of us to claim. There is no hard and fast definition of success. The notion of success comes from within; it means different things to different people. The young woman from Nantucket might define success as a happy marriage and a home in the country. The old man from Harlem might define success as being at peace with God. The immigrant from Cuba might define success as liberty and the pursuit of happiness. The orphan child from Malawi might define success as being cared for and loved. Each of us is responsible for shaping his or her own definition of what it means to be successful.

Defining success requires a deep understanding of our most intimate needs. It is an inward journey with many dimensions. Because we live in a capitalistic society that values accomplishment and the accumulation of wealth, many of us base our definition of success on fame, fortune, social status and material possessions. It is difficult to escape the superficial images of success perpetuated daily by the mass media. We cannot read a magazine or newspaper without feeling the influence of glossy advertisements, which define success based on luxury goods and designer products. However, this is a shortsighted definition of success.

For those of us who are involved with family matters and raising children, the definition of success is often expressed vicariously, through the success of our children. We live for the day when our children will grow up and make something of themselves, so that we can claim their success as ours. More unsettling are people whose definition of success is based on the level of acceptance and approval they receive from others. Many of us place a high premium on being part of the right crowd. Without serious introspection and inner work, it is hard to overcome such misguided images of success.

Success in life requires that we be grounded in something more substantial than attaining material wealth, living vicariously through our children or winning the approval and acceptance of others. A more accurate measure of success is whether we are using our lives to promote ideals, principles and values that can benefit humanity, whether we are following our dreams and passions, and whether we are striving to be the best persons possible. Ralph Waldo Emerson said it best when he observed the following:

He has achieved success
    who has lived well,
    laughed often, and loved much;
who has enjoyed the trust of pure women,
    the respect of intelligent men
    and the love of little children;
who has filled his niche and accomplished his task;
who has left the world better than he found it
    whether by an improved poppy,
    a perfect poem, or a rescued soul;
who has never lacked appreciation of Earth's
    beauty or failed to express it;
who has always looked for the best in others
    and given them the best he had;
whose life was an inspiration;
whose memory a benediction.

The meaning of success is not constant; rather it changes as our needs change. My friend, Anita, shared with me that when she was in her twenties, success meant completing her education, finding a spouse and raising a family. In her forties, it meant having a rewarding and meaningful career. Now that she is in her sixties, she defines success as maintaining her health and having peace of mind. Our characterization of success evolves as we do.

Regardless of how we define success, it does not come overnight. Like a child, success requires nurturing. It is the result of hard work, persistence, determination, sacrifice, commitment and faith. Although there is no guarantee that our road to success will be paved in gold, all of us have the inner capacity to reach our chosen destination.

Keepsake

Success is a state of mind, not just an outcome. The best measure of success is happiness.

The Power of Choice

*Life is an endlessly creative experience, and
we are shaping ourselves at every moment
by every decision we make.*

— Kent Nerburn

How we travel through life is our choice. We can choose to travel in fear or in faith. We can travel with heavy baggage from our past or we can travel lightly, having only the present before us. We can travel aimlessly without any direction, or we can travel on a well-defined course with a clear sense of purpose. We can travel on a narrow path of conformity and mediocrity or we can travel on a wide path of self-discovery and understanding.

We control our destiny by the choices we make. When we wake up each morning, we are faced with myriad choices. Aside from the decisions of what to eat for breakfast or what to wear to work, we have the awesome responsibility of choosing our course in life. Our choices define who we are; each decision we make is an opportunity for personal growth and a deliberate step toward understanding our true essence.

Every day we are called upon to make choices that shape our lives. Should I go to work? Should I end the relationship? How should I raise my children? Should I ask for a promotion? However simple or complex our choices may be, they are acts of self-expression that force us to live life intentionally and purposefully. Finding the courage to make choices is to acquire tremendous power. Without the ability to choose, we cannot realize our true potential.

Life is a series of choices. Few circumstances in life are so definite that they cannot be changed. It is unnecessary to trudge through life in an unfulfilling job, an unhealthy relationship or other situations that compromise our happiness. We have the power at any time to choose a different path. Whether we choose to stay in a bad marriage or get a divorce is our choice. Whether we choose to toil in an unrewarding job or pursue other opportunities is our choice. Whether we choose to wallow in self-pity and defeat or pick ourselves up and march toward victory is our choice. All of us are intrinsically free to do as we please; at anytime we can intervene and change our course. Even in situations beyond our control, we can choose how we allow them to affect us. Life is lived from the inside out. We cannot always change the world around us, but we can change the world within us.

A fundamental requirement for making choices is knowing what we want. Life-sustaining choices cannot be made in a vacuum. Unless we know what our heart desires, we cannot move forward. Being clear about what we want helps eliminate the influences of others from our decision-making process. Clarity allows us to take stock of ourselves and trust our own instincts. Once we are clear, we can move forward with the conviction that the universe is on our side and will lead us down the most desirable path.

Many of us dread making choices because of their high stakes and serious consequences. We are afraid that we will fail or make the wrong decision. Every choice we make requires a leap of faith. There is no guarantee that our choice will produce the outcome we expect. But each exercise of choice teaches us more about ourselves. Life is a process of growth, and our ability to choose is fundamental to what we learn. The only way we can grow is by taking the risk that our choices will enlighten us and make us more aware of who we are. Exercising our right to choose moves us closer to manifesting our destiny.

A fascinating story in philosopher Swami Chetanananda's *Choose to Be Happy* illustrates the power of choice in our lives. In the story, a woman reaches the edge of a vast river and realizes that she has just enough material to build one of two things: a cottage in which to settle down or a raft on which to explore new worlds. Rain is pouring at the river's edge, and her first impulse is to build a shelter and stay put. But beyond the stormy river is a distant horizon lit by a fine line of unbroken light beneath the gray-black clouds — a chance for a bold and different adventure.

The critical question we must ask ourselves is whether our goal is to build a cottage or a raft. When we come to the edge of our river, do we build a cottage for shelter and protection, or do we build a raft to take us to that unbroken line of light where new possibilities await us? The decision is not easy; however, we have the choice and the power to choose. Freedom of choice is a liberating force. It can take us anyplace we desire. We create the world we will experience through the choices we make.

Keepsake

There are no good or bad choices. Choices are simply expressions of life that help you to grow. Every choice you make expands your horizon and moves you closer to your true destiny. The path you choose today creates the life you will lead tomorrow.

Recognize Your Potential

Each of us has the potential to do something meaningful with our life. We are born with an enormous capacity to love, think, build and create. The harshest circumstances cannot hold us back when we are determined to go forward. There are no boundaries to our compassion, our intellect or our enthusiasm for life. The only thing that limits us is the stretch of our imagination. The potential within us is greater than we realize: we can be or do anything we desire.

All around us are examples of ordinary people who have relied on the power of their inner strengths to transform their lives. A few years ago while vacationing at a resort in the Dominican Republic, I met eight-year-old Hector. He sold wooden carvings and beaded bracelets on the beach. Although his native language was Spanish, when Hector approached me, he asked me in fluent English if I wanted to buy a carving or bracelet. He told me that he was trying to earn enough money to help care for his sick mother. I bought two wooden ashtrays and a bracelet.

Hector was an intelligent and charming little boy, and I did not find anything unusual about our encounter. However, as I observed Hector approach other people on the beach, I noticed that he spoke several languages. Most of the people at the resort were from France, Germany, Italy or some other European country. When Hector came near me again, I asked him how many languages he spoke. He replied, "Five: German, French, Italian, English and Spanish." I was impressed. Hector explained that he had taught himself the different languages so he could sell his carvings to American and European tourists who vacationed at the resort. Unless he was able to communicate with everyone, he felt that he would lose sales and not be able to help his mother.

Hector touched my heart. His story is a perfect example of the human potential that lies within each of us. We possess an amazing ability to rise and meet any challenge life presents. As Hector demonstrated, our potential is limitless. Many of us have hidden talents and abilities that we have yet to discover. The measure of our success depends on our ability to recognize and unleash our potential. Like flower bulbs, our lives will never bloom until our capacity for growth is triggered. Once we realize our human potential, our lives can blossom in any direction.

Recognizing our potential requires that we have the faith that we can expand and grow. Faith is believing in our personal power and trusting that we have everything we need to thrive. Faith in ourselves makes it possible for us to go beyond our limitations. It removes all fear and doubt from our lives and gives us the courage to dwell in new and unfamiliar places. With faith on our side, we are more inclined to move out of our comfort zones and risk being who we are.

Realizing our potential also requires openness. We must always be ready, willing and open to the wide range of possibilities life offers. The theologian Howard Thurman wrote, "The place where a man stands is never quite the place that marks the limit of his powers and resting point of his dreams." At any moment, our lives can transform into something greater than we imagined.

Greatness awaits each of us. Our job is to claim it and make it happen. We may never rise to the fame of humanitarians like Mother Theresa or Martin Luther King, Jr. or learn to speak five languages as Hector does, but each of us has boundless potential to express who we are.

Keepsake

The potential to grow, expand and create is the fiber of who you are. You can become or achieve anything you desire. Your potential is as great as your aspiration.

Build Self-Esteem

Healthy self-esteem is as essential to our survival as the air we breathe. Self-esteem is an important building block of our being. Everything we do in life is filtered through our self-esteem. Self-esteem gives us the confidence to live our dreams, set boundaries, take risks, enter and exit relationships, surrender our past, be ourselves and meet the challenges of life. In a very real sense, it is the essence of who we are. Strong self-esteem can mean the difference between a life of despair and self-doubt or a life of happiness and self-confidence. Because self-esteem plays such a prominent role in our lives, it is essential to understand how it works.

In short, self-esteem is simply how we feel and think about ourselves. It is a measure of our self-worth and value. A person with low self-esteem has little faith in himself or his abilities. He is someone who dwells on the negative aspects of life, where there is little hope. On the other hand, a person with strong self-esteem is able to see all the potential and possibility life has to offer. From his point of view, there is no limitation or obstacle that one cannot overcome.

The level of self-esteem that we experience is determined by our thoughts. Our thought process influences how we perceive ourselves, which shapes our self-image. When we think of ourselves in a positive manner — "I am beautiful," "I am healthy," "I am self-sufficient" — our self-esteem increases. If you look in the mirror and think, "I look great," this affirming thought will instantly boost your self-esteem; however, if you look in the mirror and think, "I look lousy," such negative thinking will undermine your self-esteem. The image in the mirror is the same, but our interpretation of what we see affects how we feel.

To raise our level of self-esteem we have to monitor our thoughts constantly. Negative thoughts of inferiority, hopelessness, unworthiness and self-pity are destructive and should be replaced with positive thoughts of self-love, respect and trust. The types of messages we send ourselves determine our self-perception.

After nine years of marriage, my neighbor, Troy, asked his wife Imelda for a divorce. Nothing could have prepared Imelda for the devastation she felt. The news hit her like a blunt object. Immediately, she blamed herself for Troy's dissatisfaction with their marriage. She questioned her physical attractiveness, sexual appeal, cooking habits and other aspects of life that she felt could explain Troy's rejection.

Because Imelda's identity was connected to being married to Troy, she could not imagine being without him. Even after the divorce was final and the possibility of reconciliation hopeless, she continued to blame herself for not being a better wife. It took Imelda several years to rebuild her self-esteem and realize that she had lost herself in someone else. Although the divorce was a painful experience, it forced Imelda to acknowledge her own intrinsic value. As time passed, she became able to develop a sense of self-worth and take possession of her life without the need to be attached to and defined by someone else.

We are our most valuable assets. When we view ourselves with respect, we are able to live more balanced and productive lives. Rather than being guided by fears of inadequacy and rejection, we are able to approach life with confidence. Our self-esteem is enhanced when we make accurate and honest assessments of our strengths and weaknesses, learn to recognize our abilities and talents, and acknowledge and take pride in our achievements.

For most, developing healthy self-esteem is a lifetime process, which must be carefully nurtured. Our perception or interpretation of every situation we encounter has the potential to raise or lower our self-esteem. An insensitive comment or annoyed look can erode our self-esteem; just as easily, a word of praise or a kind gesture can build it. The important lesson to remember is that we are created in the image of God. No judgment against us or act we commit can diminish our true worth.

Keepsake

Believe in yourself! Have faith in your abilities! Take pride in who you are and what you have accomplished. A sense of self-worth is critical to happiness and success. Never let the opinions of others determine your value.

Practice Self-Discipline

Self-discipline requires much more than setting an alarm clock and getting up at a designated time. Self-discipline is an ongoing, rigorous effort to control and exercise efficiency in human behavior. In more practical terms, it is the ability to follow through on our goals with faith and determination. Self-discipline is important because it keeps us centered and focused on our purpose. It defines who we are and determines who we might become.

Exercising self-discipline can be a formidable challenge. Many forces compete for our attention on a daily basis. The demands of work, the needs of family, our personal urges and desires and numerous activities distract us constantly, slowly pulling us away from our dreams. Even so, to get the results we desire in life, we have to make certain sacrifices and choices. Whether it is controlling our appetite, our spending habits or how much time we watch television, we have to commit ourselves to doing what is necessary to achieve our goals.

There is no shortage of stories about talented and brilliant people who have squandered their potential because they lacked self-discipline. Do you remember the fable, *The Ant and the Grasshopper*? The ant works hard in the scorching heat all summer, building his house and storing supplies for the winter. The grasshopper laughs at the ant and thinks he is a fool; instead of preparing for the winter, the grasshopper spends his summer dancing and playing the fiddle. Finally, winter arrives and the ant is warm and well fed. The grasshopper has no food or shelter, so he is left in the cold. The moral of the story is that all of us must exercise self-control and take responsibility for our well-being. It is not enough to be endowed naturally with special talents and abilities. Self-discipline and commitment are required to harness and refine our talents, and to reach our full potential.

Although self-discipline is one of the most reliable ways of assuring success, it is often viewed with skepticism. Some have the misconception that self-discipline takes away our freedom and prevents us from enjoying the pleasures of life. On the contrary, self-discipline enhances our quality of life. By minimizing idle and unproductive behavior, self-discipline helps us to focus our attention on more worthwhile pursuits. When we are disciplined, we are more likely to follow through with our dreams and aspirations. One of the most satisfying rewards in life comes when we work hard to achieve a specific goal and attain it.

Self-discipline is not limited to our physical actions. We must also discipline the way we think. In *Everyday Grace*, Marianne Williamson writes, "Our greatest weakness is the weakness of an undisciplined mind." Our thoughts create our reality. It is counterproductive to regulate our physical movement while our thoughts are left uncensored. Thoughts are potent forces. We create our circumstances, surroundings and destiny in life by how we think. In order to control our lives it is vital to control our thinking. A disciplined mind is a precursor to personal growth.

The value of self-discipline in our lives is immeasurable. The best way to avoid situations in life that hurl us into the fray and distract us from our purpose is to exercise self-control. By maintaining order and focus and by remaining steadfast in our pursuits, life can be as fulfilling and rewarding as we desire.

Keepsake

Self-discipline increases your ability to achieve and sustain success. To progress you need a sense of order, control and structure in your life. Self-discipline is the foundation for achieving all hopes and dreams.

Attitude Is Everything

Life flows unpredictably. Our days seldom unfold as we expect. On any given day, we have no control over a large portion of what happens to us. Every day is a journey into the unknown. From getting caught in a violent storm off the Gulf of Mexico, as the victims of Hurricane Katrina were, to inheriting a large sum of money from an unexpected source, anything is possible. Only God knows what path we will take.

Although we cannot control most of the circumstances of our lives, we *can* control how we react to them. Our attitude determines how we interpret and interact with the world and how the world reacts to us. All of us are familiar with the proverbial half-full/half-empty glass of water approach to life: the glass can be viewed as half-full or half-empty depending on our point of view. Our perspective is determined by our attitude, which is the mental process though which we view reality. Therefore, how we react to circumstances in life is our decision. Our response is a deliberate choice. By simply adjusting our attitude, we can look at a situation in a positive or negative light. This is not to suggest that we should manipulate our thinking the way the storybook character Pollyanna does; she chooses to see everything through rose-colored glasses. We do not need to deceive ourselves. But it is important to realize that we have the power to control our perceptions. Regardless of how hopeless or unfortunate a situation is perceived to be, the quality of our attitude determines how we are affected. A good attitude is the ability to maintain a positive outlook, even in the gloomiest situation.

My first job out of law school was with a firm in Pittsburgh. After graduation, I anxiously moved to Pittsburgh to start my new career as a corporate attorney. I had always dreamed of being a high-powered attorney in a blue chip firm. Since the sixth grade, I had visualized dressing in navy blue and pinstriped suits, wearing wire-framed eyeglasses and carrying a thick leather briefcase.

Once at the firm, however, it did not take me long to realize that my dream did not match reality and would not materialize as I expected. The work assignments were mundane, the environment was unpleasant, and to make matters worse, the winters in Pittsburgh were unbearably cold. Rather than complaining and focusing on the negative aspects of the job, I adjusted my attitude and used the experience as an opportunity to sharpen my legal skills, while I searched for a new job. I eventually found a more rewarding job with a non-profit organization that provided college scholarships to disadvantaged students. However, my job experience in Pittsburgh taught me invaluable lessons in faith and perseverance.

Although it is not always apparent, there is usually a silver lining in every cloud that obscures our view. Sometimes we just have to look beyond the surface to find it. All of us have been in situations that initially did not seem promising, but when we changed our attitude about them, they became tolerable.

Each of us has the power to determine how and to what extent we are served by a situation. Losing a job may be perceived as a failure, or as an opportunity to do something more rewarding. A gray, overcast day may be viewed with gloom or delight. Our feelings about a situation depend on our perspective. Sometimes in situations that seem troubling or beyond hope, all that is necessary is a change of attitude. When we are able to adjust our attitude and learn to look at situations more neutrally, we usually discover that they are neither as stressful nor as difficult as they may have seemed.

Attitude is the barometer of life. It is an internal gauge that we can use to keep our lives in balance. Everything depends on our attitude toward ourselves and the world. We create our reality with our attitude. If we are pessimistic about life and transmit a negative attitude, people will avoid us. On the other hand, if we take an optimistic approach to life and transmit a positive attitude, people will embrace us.

If you want to change the circumstances of your life, the first step is to change your attitude. By thinking positively and making an effort to learn from our experiences, we can change what we perceive to be bad experiences into good experiences. A positive attitude is essential for lasting happiness, prosperity and success.

Keepsake

Approach life with a winning attitude. Take charge of how you think and feel about your life. Believe you are capable of creating the life you desire.

Insist on Being Yourself

Such as I am, I am a precious gift.
— Zora Neal Hurston

Each of us represents the beauty and uniqueness of life. The combination of our genes, cells, muscle tissues, talent and DNA is unlike that of any other person on earth. There is no one else anywhere in the world who looks like us, walks the way we walk, smiles the way we smile, dances the way we dance or thinks the way we think. Each of us also has a special mission, a story to tell or a song to sing. Everyone is unique in both appearance and purpose. The only debt we owe the world is to be ourselves.

Although being ourselves is the most natural thing any of us can do, we often make it difficult. We do not feel comfortable in our own skin. Rather than embrace our individuality and uniqueness, many of us suppress our true nature. We hide behind appearances and pretend to be something we are not.

The best solution to peace and contentment is to be authentic. True happiness comes from genuine self-expression. Life demands that we exclude nothing of ourselves from the world. There is no shrinking back into the shadows. We are expected to show up on the world's stage every day and to reveal passionately, honestly and openly who we are — to show it all, to offer ourselves in every way possible, even to reveal the pain and scars that many of us are tempted to mask.

When we yearn to be other than who we are, we lose our identity in the process. Instead of comparing ourselves to others or trying to live up to their expectations, we must insist on being ourselves. We must be willing to stand on firm ground and announce to the world, "I am who I am." There is no room for compromise. Our role has been cast by the divine will of God.

Following the expectations of others compromises our ability to be ourselves. It is essential that the path we choose in life is a reflection of our own hopes, dreams and aspirations, and not those of our parents, spouses or friends. Each of us is blessed with unique talents and attributes that only we can bring to fruition.

The key to embracing our true essence is acceptance. Acceptance is the fundamental principle of personal growth. We cannot become whole by resisting who we are. Acceptance means being okay with who we are, exactly as we are right now. It means that we acknowledge, experience and accept our situations in life as uniquely ours. There are specific qualities about each of us that cannot be changed. They are a natural part of who we are. The face we are born with is the face we must carry with us throughout our entire life. Our feet cannot be exchanged like a pair of shoes. The sound of our voice, the twinkle in our eyes, the size of our waist, the drape of our arms, the bend of our knees and the texture of our hair make us who we are. Whether we love it or hate it, accept it or reject it, our bodies belong to us for life. It is vital to our well-being that we accept every aspect of our being with a positive and loving spirit.

Self-acceptance provides a healthy foundation for being ourselves. It is also essential for self-loving. As I mentioned before, practicing the art of self-love requires us to accept ourselves completely as we are. Regardless of our physical traits, we must be completely comfortable with who we are. Any attempt to hide or disguise our true nature diminishes our value. Our contribution to humanity relies on our courage to be ourselves.

Acceptance is not limited to our physical characteristics. We have to accept everything about ourselves including our thoughts and feelings, the troubling choices we have made, an unfavorable past, and our faults and shortcomings. The true value of acceptance is that it makes us feel better about ourselves, and it helps us to experience reality without self-reproach. By accepting everything about ourselves — even the things we do not like — peace can become manifest in our lives.

When we accept ourselves as we are, the need for external validation ends. We can move beyond our insecurities and let life unfold on a natural course of self-discovery. At this stage in life, we are at our height of creativity and spiritual development. Although occasionally we may be inclined to look beyond ourselves for answers and understanding, we know our greatest strengths are embedded in our own heads, hearts and souls. Self-acceptance allows us to build our future on the basis of who we are instead of condemning ourselves for who we are not.

Keepsake

Dare to be yourself. You possess a combination of unique traits, talents and abilities that only you can bring to fruition. The way to find fulfillment and peace in the world is to be your authentic self. Once you accept who you are, you can embrace all aspects of human experience.

The Path to Happiness

*Happiness is like perfume; you can't pour it on somebody
else without getting a few drops on yourself.*

— James Van Der Zee

.

Like other choices we make every day, if we want
happiness, we must choose it. Nothing else is
required. As astounding as it may seem, we already have
embedded within us everything we need to be happy.
No magical formula, external condition or ideal situation, event or person exists that will suddenly make our
lives wonderful. Genuine happiness comes from inside.
It is always within our grasp. We just have to open our
hearts to the possibility of being happy.

In her book *Dying to Live: A Call to Joy,* my friend
Natalie Taylor writes about how a life-threatening ill-
ness changed her life and helped her to find happiness.
A few years ago, Natalie discovered that a large tumor

had grown between her rectum and spine, forcing her vital organs out of alignment. The diagnosis made sense of the severe pain she had been experiencing for several months. Facing the possibility of death, Natalie immediately underwent surgery to remove the tumor. Although struggling with the illness was difficult, she writes that it also was the most "joyful" experience of her life. According to Natalie, the illness was a "wake-up call," it was her "mountain top call to joy," because it helped her to fully appreciate her blessings, including being alive, which ultimately became her *inner* source of joy.

Some of us are so accustomed to looking for happiness in the wrong places that we are unsure of what it means to be truly happy. Happiness is a state of mind. It is a disposition of optimism and joy that permeates our entire being. It is not something someone brings to us on a silver platter. Happiness is characterized by feelings of gratitude, inner peace, satisfaction and affection for others and ourselves. When we are happy, there is a feeling *inside* that everything is all right. We feel euphoric. We whistle as we walk down the street, and we experience internal feelings of gladness.

Often we underestimate our capacity for real happiness. Rather than looking inward, we tend to base our happiness on external triggers. We fantasize that once we get married, graduate from college, buy a new house, lose weight, find a job or attain some other goal, our lives will be complete and we will live happily ever after. These fantasies only polish the surface. Happiness is an internal response. It is not contingent on the occurrence of future events or the acquisition of certain objects. Happiness based on external conditions is superficial and cannot be sustained. The moment we achieve the desired object of happiness, we change our standard, and something else becomes the new object of our happiness.

Happiness is a feeling, not an outcome. There is a difference between "being" happy about something and "feeling" happy. At some point in our lives, we all have declared, "I will be so happy when … (a certain condition is met)," only to realize later that satisfying the condition did not bring us the level of happiness we anticipated. When I finished law school and passed the bar exam, I thought becoming an attorney would be my answer to happiness. To my dismay, I did not feel the sensation I expected. Within months of being admitted to the bar, I had begun to create new conditions for happiness.

My experience was not different from that of my friend, Charlotte, who planned a beautiful wedding and got married with the assumption that marriage would make her happy. We both learned that the completion of desired events does not guarantee happiness. This type of happiness is elusive. True happiness flows from within us.

We simply cannot rely on people, places, events or other circumstances to bring us happiness. Happiness is independent of external circumstances. The fact that we are alive and well is reason enough to feel happy. Happiness is our birthright; it is a state of consciousness that already exists within us. There is nothing we can do on the outside to sustain our happiness on the inside. Authentic happiness is cultivated from within. We have to learn to be happy simply as we are.

Keepsake

Happiness can only be found within. You are the source of your own happiness. Do not wait for others to bring happiness to you. You already have everything you need to be happy.

PART TWO

Sacred
Communions

*Every time we come in contact with
another person we experience a
sacred communion. With each encounter
our lives are spiritually, emotionally and
mentally transformed. There is an
exchange of energy, love and wisdom
that deepens our understanding of
the world and ourselves.*

Give from the Heart

From what we get, we can make a living; what we give,
however, makes a life.

— Arthur Ashe

Although many of us place a premium on the things
we receive, it is what we give that really matters.
Giving is a natural and expected consequence of life.
Whether it is a cool drink of water on a warm day or
help with paying a bill, we all depend on the kindness,
consideration and charity of one another. Life is a series
of small gestures, a way of connecting with others and
showing gratitude for our blessings. There is no one on
earth whose life has not been touched by the generosity
of another person.

Before she died, Mother Theresa left us with the sen-
timent, "The greatest good is what we do for each other."
Personal growth, love, compassion and abundance are

all part of the cycle of giving. It is a universal law: what we give is what we receive.

Giving is most powerful when it comes from the heart. It is an inward desire to reach out and help someone in need. When you look back on your life, consider what has given you the most satisfaction: Graduating from college? Moving from your parents' house to your own apartment? Purchasing your first car? A promotion at work? Or something you did to help someone else?

I read a remarkable story in the newspaper about a mailman who randomly selects people who need help and sends them gifts of one thousand dollars through the mail. The motive for his generosity is simply the feeling of joy in giving. There are no strings attached to his kindness. He gives from his heart. As the mailman can attest, it is our impulse to give that enriches our lives most. Believing that we are helpful to others makes the difference between merely existing and living fully.

Opportunities to give are plentiful. Giving can be done in the form of a donation to a large charity like Oprah's Angel Network or the Habitat for Humanity, a basket of fruit delivered to a sick person in the hospital or tutoring a child. The act of giving can even be as simple as sharing homemade peach preserves with your neighbors — something my neighbor did every summer when I was a child growing up in Arkansas. Giving says to the universe, "I believe there is enough." Sacrificial giving says to the universe, "I trust you." In each case, the universe sends us circumstances that reinforce these messages. There are no special guidelines for giving. The only requirement is a willingness to open our hearts for the well-being of others.

When we think of giving, most of us tend to think about large gifts that are donated by rich people, like the twenty million dollar gift Bill and Camille Cosby gave to Spelman College or the one billion dollar pledge Ted Turner made to the United Nations. It is a misconception to believe that we must be rich to give. The mailman is an example of modest means. Delivering mail is his only source of income. Even so, through his altruistic spirit and willingness to share, he has been able to make a tremendous difference in the lives of the people he touches.

Giving is not always about money. All of us, regardless of the size of our incomes or bank accounts, have a wealth of inner resources that we can share with others. We can give attention, smiles, prayers, love, respect, humor and hope. We can offer a word of encouragement or a shoulder to lean on. Our capacity for giving is enormous.

One evening when I was leaving work, a homeless man approached me with his hands clasped and asked if I had any spare change. I was predisposed to say "No." Instead, I asked him what he intended to do with the money. He replied, "Buy an ice cream cone." His un-expected response tickled my heart. How could I deny him such a simple pleasure? I bought ice cream for us both. This experience taught me to give simply for the fun of it.

Each of us should make a point to give something of ourselves each day. By enriching the lives of others with our love and generosity, we make ourselves more susceptible to the blessings of the universe.

Keepsake

Giving is an unselfish act of love. Commit to giving something every day. You can give time, attention or a kind word. The measure of your life is not what you receive, but what you give. In every aspect of life, the more you give the more you will gain.

Embrace the Truth

*Take a day to heal from the lies you've told yourself and
from the ones that have been told to you.*

— Maya Angelou

The truth is always present. Regardless of how hard
we may try, we cannot escape the truth. Like a
constant companion, it is with us everywhere we go. It
lingers in the rafters of our homes. It crouches beneath
our dashboards. It canvasses the corridors of our job
sites. It lubricates our relationships. It rings in the towers
of our churches. Truth exists everywhere, all the time, in
everything. It dwells in every aspect of our lives.

Our challenge relates to how we deal with the truth.
Most of us handle the truth like a fragile package. We
do not know whether to caress it gently or place it aside;
whether to guard it with our lives or set it free; whether
to live with it or deny it; whether to whisper it softly or

59

proclaim it to the world. The truth can also be a heavy and burdensome load to carry. It can hurt and disappoint us, ruin good intentions or bring the wrath of others upon us. Regardless of the consequences, start today to embrace the truth. To witness the truth, to speak it, to feel it is like being reborn. It delivers us out of darkness into light.

Truth can be expressed in many ways. Our first obligation is to be true to ourselves. Like the flow of our blood, every thought we think, word we speak and choice we make should come from the heart, the source of all truth.

Living from the heart is one of the greatest challenges of life. Living from the heart requires us to be honest about who we are and how we feel. Living from the heart means that we approach our relationships with openness and integrity. Living from the heart is allowing the spirit of God to flow through us. Every time we exercise the truth, we clear the way for greater understanding, love and harmony to enter our lives. Truth is a peacemaker and a healer. It makes it possible for us to negotiate the world with a clear conscience and a pure heart.

We also have a moral obligation to be honest with those around us. One of the most valuable lessons we are taught as children is to tell the truth. As we grow older, we tend to lose our penchant for honesty. In a world filled with deceit, lies and hypocrisy, however, the truth is our last beacon of hope. It resolves conflict, restores order and brings a sense of reality and certainty into our lives. According to the author Iyanla Vanzant, truth is the foundation of all spiritual principles and the light that illuminates all knowing. Without truth as a guide, we cannot move forward.

Most of us avoid the truth because we are afraid that we will be ostracized or rejected, or we fear it will destroy the delicate fabric of our relationships. Ironically, to keep harmony we adopt a policy of stretching or coloring the truth. Instead of being honest with our friends and loved ones, we tell them what we believe they want to hear. A classic example is when a friend asks our opinion about a new dish she has prepared and we tell her it taste delicious to protect her feelings. Ultimately, denying the truth does more harm than good. Foremost, it compromises our personal sense of integrity. It also denies others the benefit of an honest opinion.

Although it is sometimes difficult, telling the truth is always a positive and worthwhile experience. Truth is our greatest desire, our friend, our common ground, our liberator. Facing the truth is the only way we can change and grow. The more truth that exists in our lives, the freer we are.

Just as important as telling the truth is how we tell it. The truth should be spoken as gently and as sweetly as we sing praises. Truthfulness is the path to understanding and empowerment. It is a shield of protection, not a weapon of destruction. The more graciously we are able to handle the truth, the more beautifully our lives will unfold.

Keepsake

Pursue truth with fervor. It is the safest ground on which to stand.

Master the Art of Friendship

A friend gathers all the pieces and
gives them back in the right order.

— Toni Morrison

I once knew a woman who earned a living making quilts. Her quilting style was bold and distinct like an abstract painting. She used the patchwork technique: patched-together pieces of fabric in geometric shapes that are tightly stitched into a particular pattern. I learned that a key factor in quilt-making is the quality of the fabrics used to make the patches and the type of stitching used to hold them together. According to her, the more exotic, colorful and varied the fabrics, the more beautiful the quilt.

Making quilts is like making friends. Both processes require strong bonds and gentle care. The tighter, more loving, more caring and more colorful our friends are, the more meaningful and fulfilling our lives can be. Good friends add warmth, happiness, understanding, perspective and purpose to the woven patterns of our lives. We all need human bonding and intimacy to thrive.

Friends help us capture and celebrate the many dimensions of life. They rejoice in our triumphs, provide comfort when we are hurt and offer clarity when we are confused. The greatest benefit of having friends is that they allow us to be ourselves. Few experiences are more valuable than the time we spend with friends, talking and reflecting over the wonders of life. Friendship is a collaborative process of shared moments — moments of happiness, moments of pain, moments of hope, moments of laughter and moments of affection. The special moments we share make life worth living.

There is no secret formula for attracting and meeting friends. The potential to develop a friendship exists wherever two people cross paths, whether at work, in the library, on the subway or at church; while walking through the park or sunbathing on the beach. My cousin, Tammie, met her best friend, Donnie (who later became her husband), at a stoplight in Tulsa. Just before the light changed, he was able to invite her on a date. Opportunities to meet friends are numerous. The only requirement is being open to the possibility of friendship. Even so, friendship does not come easily.

Most of us can count the number of friends we have on one hand. For a friendship to flourish, it must be nurtured constantly and massaged. The poet Ralph Waldo Emerson wrote, "The only way to have a friend is to be one." To win and keep friends, all of us must master the art of friendship.

Building and maintaining friendships require honesty, understanding, communication, a caring attitude and an ability to listen. Friendships also require constant repair. To sustain them, there must be frequent and open communication. We must take the time to call, write a note, meet for lunch or send a gift on special occasions. A willingness to reach out to one another is paramount.

Friendships that span time are like mountain ranges that cover long distances: they have peaks and valleys. A true measure of friendship is the ability to endure the rough times, as well as the good times. According to the philosopher Seneca, "A firm and gentle friendship … sweetens our cares, dispels our sorrows and counsels us in extremities." A loving and caring friendship is our best hope for tomorrow. Just as the fabric in a beautiful patchwork quilt cannot hold together without tight stitching, no soul can maneuver along the winding path of life without a true friend.

Keepsake

You must be as careful about keeping friends as you are about making them.

Cultivate Compassion

*True compassion is more
than throwing a coin to a beggar.*
— Dr. Martin Luther King, Jr.

Compassion is our most endearing form of human interaction. It is the ability to respond to another person's pain and suffering with an overwhelming desire to offer comfort. Showing compassion toward one another is fundamental to human existence. Compassion is the link that connects and comforts us, and helps us transcend our most painful experiences.

Regardless of how hard we try to maintain balance and control over our lives, each of us will eventually need the comfort of a compassionate heart. As human beings, potential for pain, hurt and suffering looms ever-present. It is unrealistic to think we can triumph in life without the goodwill of those around us. Compassion is the greatest support we can show each other.

Compassion involves more than giving money or offering kind words. It requires direct contact and interaction with the person who is suffering. We must be willing to give our time and loving attention. The surrender of *self* is what makes a difference in a person's life. Compassion is a conscious effort to open our hearts and actually feel another person's pain. It is not enough to drop a coin in a homeless person's cup and walk away. To show compassion we must be willing to sit with, talk to and hold the hand of someone who is suffering. The unselfish act of compassion soothes and heals a heavy heart.

Although most of us believe we can handle any situation, we are rarely prepared when misfortune crosses our path. My friend, Sophia, told me a tragic story about her neighbor, Loretta, who was evicted from her home four days after she was diagnosed with breast cancer. Upon hearing the news, Sophia felt compelled to reach out to Loretta. She invited Loretta to sleep on a sofa bed until she was able to find a new place and get back on her feet.

Unfortunately, as fate would have it, as soon as Loretta found a new apartment, appearing to rebound from her temporary setback, her health began to deteriorate. She had to undergo chemotherapy to keep the cancer from spreading. The side effects of the chemotherapy were severe. Loretta lost a tremendous amount of weight and most of her hair. Sudden and dramatic changes in appearance devastated her. To ease the pain and help Loretta regain a sense of dignity and self-worth, Sophia routinely applied Loretta's make-up and polished her nails. Sophia's heart of compassion made Loretta feel better about herself and had a therapeutic impact on her recovery.

Although Sophia was the caregiver in this situation, her life was affected as much as Loretta's was. Sophia learned to focus on the positive aspects of life and not to give much attention to superficial matters, like her wardrobe or social calendar. She also learned to live life in the moment and without regrets. Compassion enriches the life of both the person who suffers and the person who provides comfort. Treating others with tenderness and consideration is an automatic deposit in the universal bank of abundance. Even more, a compassionate heart helps us to connect with our own essence. Pathways to self-discovery and connecting with others are intertwined. Helping others enables us to form a better understanding of who we are.

Not only must we treat others with compassion, but we must also have compassion for ourselves. Treating ourselves with compassion helps us overcome the fear and self-doubt that many of us tend to harbor. Compassion makes it possible for us to see ourselves as part of a greater whole, which ultimately moves us closer to our spiritual source.

Keepsake

Offer the world compassion. But first, extend compassion to yourself.

Have the Grace to Smile

Beauty exists in everything in nature. In the flower, beauty is the splendor of the blossom. In the ocean, it is the splashing of the waves against a quiet shore. In the sun, it is the radiance of light. In the peacock, it is the kaleidoscopic span of the feathers. In the zebra, it is the pattern of the stripes. In human beings, it is the glistening of smiles. Our smile is one of our most visible attributes. It sets the tone for everything that enters our lives.

A smile is like magic. Simply by flexing a few muscles in our face we can instantly transform our lives. A smile can warm hearts, attract new friendships, change attitudes, defuse tense situations, inspire hope when circumstances appear hopeless and heal old wounds.

Wearing a smile communicates to others that we are open and willing to receive them with love and warmth. It is a perfect antidote for breaking through barriers of suspicion, intolerance and discord. Do you remember how much happiness was generated when your grade school teacher marked a smiling face on your home-work assignment? The same feeling is created when two people exchange a smile. The innocence and genuine-ness of the moment transcend our worldly cares.

Many of us avoid smiling because we feel that we do not have a reason to smile. We rationalize not smiling with the idea that things are not as they should be or as we would like them to be in our lives. Rather than live in the moment and enjoy life as it unfolds, we delude ourselves into believing that the occurrence of some future act will eventually make life worth smiling about. We tell ourselves, "I will smile when my bills are paid off," or "… when I meet the right person," or "… when I lose weight." Fortunately, a perfect life or ideal situation is not a prerequisite for smiling.

When the company that has employed you for twelve years downsizes and leaves you behind, have the grace to smile. When you feel the seams of several years of marriage start to unravel, have the grace to smile. Anytime life throws you a blow that you did not expect, have the grace to smile. Smiling is a simple gesture that lets the universe know we are open and receptive to the challenges of life. A smile may not change our immedi-ate circumstances, but it brightens our outlook on life and affirms that we are part of a divine mission that is greater than temporary setbacks.

Regardless of our present circumstances, a warm, friendly smile is always ours to give. A smile comes so easily, yet travels so far. If only we would fix our hearts so we would deliver them more often to people we encounter! By simply wearing a smile on our face, we can take the first step toward creating a world of peace.

Keepsake

The simplest way to communicate warmth and goodwill is with a smile. Even when you do not know the recipient, a smile alone can open a pathway to the heart.

Set Boundaries

Boundaries are essential for shaping a productive and successful life. They help us establish standards and principles that govern how we live and relate to others. To remain centered and focused on our divine mission, we have to set boundaries and live by them; otherwise, life can become a freewheeling adventure.

The poet Robert Frost wrote, "Good fences make good neighbors." Just as boundaries exist between neighbors, it is essential that we draw them in our personal lives. Personal boundaries separate us from the influences, beliefs and desires of others. They help us determine who is worthy of our time, attention and space. Most importantly, they allow us to take possession of our lives and live on our own terms.

Life is too precious to be taken for granted. To protect who we are and what we stand for, it is critical that we set personal boundaries and honor them. Obviously, some things suit our lives and others do not.

Setting boundaries gives us the ability to choose what is right for us. Without well-placed boundaries to keep us grounded and focused, we invite disorder and confusion into our lives, allowing ourselves to be too easily influenced or distracted from our purpose.

Personal boundaries also add depth and meaning to our relationships. They help us define the amount of trust, understanding, commitment and affection we expect from others, and make it possible for us to align ourselves with people who have a compatible outlook on life. Still, we must be careful that our boundaries are not so inflexible that they isolate us from others. Personal boundaries are meant to enhance our relationships rather than diminish them.

As a child, when I got into a feud or dispute with one of the children in my neighborhood, someone would draw a line in the dirt between us. If either of us became bold enough to cross the line into the other person's space, a fistfight would ensue. Fortunately, it is not necessary for adults to engage in such childish antics. We can establish boundaries in our lives simply by saying "yes" or "no."

There is no reason to feel guilty or apologetic about setting boundaries. Boundaries not only help others know where we stand, but they also help us preserve our values and maintain our standards. When others test our boundaries, we have a responsibility to be firm in our convictions. Even animals recognize the importance of protecting their environment. They use a variety of methods to let other animals or people know they have a particular interest in a certain space. For example, a dog will bark to drive away what he believes to be an intrusion into his territory. Similarly, a bird will swoop down aggressively toward someone who gets too close to her nest. We owe it to ourselves to be no less fervent in our effort to preserve our personal boundaries.

In addition to setting healthy boundaries for ourselves, it is crucial that we respect the boundaries of others. Sometimes a small gesture like knocking on a door before entering a room is enough to show a person that his space is respected and valued. All of us have the right to expect that our personal space will not be violated. Unless we set boundaries, we risk compromising our core beliefs, values and principles. Boundaries give us room to grow and define who we are.

Keepsake

Boundaries are not limits. They are opportunities for personal growth. To keep your value and belief systems intact, boundaries are essential.

Do a Kind Deed Daily

The smallest act of kindness is worth
more than the grandest intention.

— Unknown

"Do a kind deed daily" was a statement that my grade school teacher, Mrs. Haley, routinely made. She was determined to instill in my classmates and me a sense of caring and goodwill. Some lessons are timeless. If all of us adopted this advice as our personal mantra, the world would be a better place. Every random act of kindness we perform connects us with the essence of who we are and those around us. All of us are put on earth to make a difference in each other's lives. It is our benevolence towards each other that makes life worth living.

Acts of kindness add softness and warmth to a world that sometimes can be cold and impersonal. The effort that it takes to do a kind deed is minuscule compared to the outpouring of love and goodwill it generates.

Imagine how the little, old lady feels when someone helps her cross a busy intersection or carries her bag of groceries up a flight of stairs.

Whenever we are the beneficiaries of a kind deed, our spirits are lifted. Every door someone holds open for us, every coin a stranger places in our expired parking meter generates a positive feeling of appreciation and gratitude. Random acts of kindness enrich us beyond measure.

One day, I received an unexpected card in the mail. When I opened it, I was surprised to find my driver's license enclosed with the inscription "Found November 14th on K Street. Love, Tracey." Even before I realized my license was missing, I had been blessed by the kindness of a stranger. Such small but enduring gestures help restore our faith in one another.

Doing a kind deed not only affects the recipient in a positive and meaningful way, but it also benefits the person who performs it. Helping others allows us to deflect attention away from our own concerns and to focus on something other than ourselves. It gives us the chance to walk in another person's footsteps and experience life from a different perspective.

Any impulse we get to help another person is an opportunity to transcend personal bounds. None of us is immune to the twists and turns of life. Regardless of our present circumstances, sooner or later, we will need the comforting hands of another person. By reaching out to others, we make it possible for the same blessings to flow back to us. A few years ago, I gave my neighbor a cutting of hosta from my garden. Last summer my hosta died just as the cutting I had given my neighbor began to take form and spread. This spring, she gave me a cutting from hers. It is a fundamental truth: when we do good, some of the good we do comes back to us.

Every kind deed performed is a testament to the goodness of humanity. Regardless of the paths we choose, we all have the same desire to feel cared for and loved. A spiritual transformation occurs when two people cross paths and are able to walk away with a renewed sense of hope, peace and love.

Keepsake

Never underestimate the power of a kind gesture. Random acts of kindness are gifts of the spirit that allow you to relate to others with generosity and humility.

Resist the Temptation to Judge

*It is very easy to sit in judgment upon the behavior
of others, but often difficult to realize that
every judgment is a self-judgment.*

— Howard Thurman

More than any other influences, our relationships help to shape who we are. Every time we cross paths with another person, the opportunity for personal growth and deeper understanding abounds. Each person we meet has the potential to teach us more about ourselves and the world than we knew before. Brief encounters with people in the street, at the grocery store, on the bus, at church or sitting on a park bench, can enrich our lives in profound and meaningful ways. Even in such fleeting, unpredictable situations, it is possible to answer the deepest questions of our existence. We all possess vital information that can transform ourselves and the world.

Unfortunately, we are not always open to the possibilities that others bring to our lives. Rather than embrace people we encounter in everyday situations with an attitude of openness and acceptance, often we diminish their impact on our lives by judging them. Based on their appearance, political belief, speech pattern, skin color, body language, job title, social standing or other factors, we readily conclude that their lives add no value to our own.

"That color does not suit her." "She seems so aggressive; even worse, she smokes." This is how I judged my close and dear friend, Stephanie, when I met her. Although I had yet to have any meaningful contact with Stephanie, I was sure that her life did not complement mine. Fortunately, as I opened up and allowed myself to become better acquainted with her, I was able to look beyond my initial impression and see her as a beautiful and witty person. My rush to judgment almost sabotaged what has been a caring and enduring friendship for more than twenty years.

Ironically, an inclination to judge others is often a reflection of one's own shortcomings. Deep inside we know that we cannot live up to the standards we impose on others; therefore, we use judgment as a mask to hide our fears and insecurities. From a spiritual perspective, our duty is to love and accept others as they are. We do not have the right to judge, and no one has the right to judge us.

Preconceived judgments blind our sense of reality and logic. They prevent us from seeing people as they really are. We justify judging others on the basis that we are screening undesirable people from our lives. In our minds, judgment is an early warning or detection device that protects us against unwanted intrusions; but judgment is as harmful to us as it is to the people we judge. Every time we erect a wall to distance ourselves from others, we undermine our own potential for growth. We never know who may be able to help us on our journey. It could very well be the scantily dressed lady, or the neighbor who is having an affair. It is not our place to measure the worthiness of others against our beliefs and standards.

Before we can achieve any measure of personal growth, we have to learn to accept people as they are. Judgments and first impressions are seldom accurate. They are usually based on biased perceptions or a lack of knowledge. To understand the real essence of a person, we must first give him an opportunity to reveal his true nature.

When we are quick to judge others, we minimize ourselves. We have to accept that people are not who we want them to be or even who they seem to be. People are simply who they are. A wise person is able to look upon another and accept him without prejudice or judgment. The moment we are able to rise above judgment is the beginning of true enlightenment.

Keepsake

Of all the judgments you pass in life, the ones you pass against yourself are the most harmful. Relinquish the need to judge others and yourself. Accepting others without judgment is essential for personal growth and building strong relationships.

Learn to Say No

Learning to say no is a companion to setting boundaries. Of the many lessons life teaches us, learning to say no is one of the most difficult to grasp. We are reluctant to say no because we are afraid of disappointing or frustrating the wishes of others, especially our family, friends and lovers. Most of us want to be agreeable; we do not want others to view us as selfish or unsupportive. As a result, we often say, "Yes, sure I'll do it," to unappealing situations, rather than take a firm stance and say no.

A friend I have known for many years telephoned me one evening. After exchanging pleasantries and catching-up on the latest news about each other, he mentioned the purpose of his call. He wanted to borrow three thousand dollars to buy his girlfriend an engagement ring. I was caught completely off guard. "The nerve of him to ask me to borrow such a large sum of money!" I thought. I would never have put him in such an awkward position. Despite my reservation about loaning him the money, I did not have the heart to say no. Instead of being honest and forthright, I acquiesced. I agreed to the loan and was left brooding. Fortunately, over time he repaid the loan. The critical point, however, is that I did not feel comfortable expressing my true feelings.

Many of us make excuses rather than say no: "Sorry, I already have plans." We may beat around the bush: "I think so, but let me check my calendar." Some of us even buy time: "I'll let you know tomorrow." Then there are those of us who acquiesce rather than honor our instincts. Although our ability to say no is an effective means of drawing healthy boundaries in our lives, saying no makes us feel guilty.

The choices we make in life should be based on our dreams and passions, not on our guilt and fears. The ability to say no when it is appropriate has powerful consequences. It is an indispensable tool on our journey toward a more loving and tranquil life. We are not obligated to honor every request that comes our way. Having the courage to say no gives us the freedom to live life on our terms. It is like having a guardian angel that guides us and keeps us focused on our path.

When someone calls to borrow money, or to invite us to a social function, or to ask to spend the weekend at our place, we always have the option to decline graciously. Saying no to situations that do not appeal to us does not compromise our sense of generosity or kindness. We are in a better position than anyone else to determine what we can or cannot do.

Viewing the use of the word no as a negative response is misguided. Saying no when we sense it is the right thing to do is to our advantage. A response of "no" builds bridges rather than destroying them. By telling others no, we create space for positive change to enter our lives. A graciously placed no can save us time and money, prevent inconvenience, provide more time to spend with our families, create room in our busy schedules to pursue our interests and hobbies and give us room to grow. No empowers us. It allows us to concentrate on what we are moving toward, rather than what we are leaving behind. As long as no is part of our vocabulary, we will be in a position to make mature choices that help define and illuminate our higher calling.

Keepsake

Have the courage to say no to situations that compromise your values and beliefs. Live life on your own terms.

PART THREE

Balancing Acts

~

*Sustaining balance and inner peace is an
ongoing process. We have to strive constantly
for harmony in our relationships,
our careers, our bodies and our minds.*

Breathe Consciously

Breathing deeply makes each moment of your life a prayer.
— Susan Taylor

The silent expansion and contraction in our chest as we breathe occurs without us thinking about it. For many, breathing is merely an involuntary response of the body that moves oxygen into the blood and carries carbon dioxide out of the body. However, there is more to breathing than its function of keeping us alive.

Everything we do in life emanates from breathing. Breathing is a remarkable source of power, which can lead to self-awareness and inner growth. It is the life force of our existence. By consciously controlling and monitoring our breathing, we can transform our lives. How we think, feel and act is determined by how we breathe. Close your eyes for a moment and sit upright. Turn your attention to your breath. Become aware of your breathing as you inhale and exhale. Experience the body expanding as you breathe in and contracting as you breathe out. One conscious breath can be more powerful than a gust of wind.

Whenever we shift our attention to the intricacies of breathing, we automatically widen our path of awareness and capacity for enlightenment. Every breath we take has the potential to unlock the immense reservoir of creativity, intelligence, truth, imagination and wisdom that lies deep within our subconscious mind, where the soul and spirit dwell. By taking us to a new and higher level of consciousness, breathing increases our spectrum of possibilities. Focusing on the passage of air through our bodies awakens us from complacency in life and forces us to take a closer look at ourselves in our most primal state. By separating us from our feelings, our thoughts and the external world, conscious breathing propels us to face our true nature.

Ultimately, we can expand our narrow sense of self and live from the wholeness of life by remembering to breathe. When you feel that your life is not going as you expected, *breathe*. When you find yourself frustrated and distressed and life becomes a struggle, *breathe*. When you need inspiration just to get through the day, *breathe*. When you meet the woman or man of your dreams and you are enjoying the euphoria of being in love, *breathe*. When a trusted friend betrays your confidence, *breathe*. When you feel you have finally learned the lessons your past experiences have been trying to teach you, *breathe*.

When we are able to breathe through the painful and euphoric experiences of life, we provide an opening for change and, ultimately, personal growth.

Contemplating breath is tantamount to contemplating life itself. With every inhalation and exhalation, the question *Who am I?* beckons for an answer. While focusing on our breath, we are able to calm down and see aspects of our lives more clearly and, subsequently, understand them more deeply. Conscious breathing forces everything into the open. The hidden corners of our lives that we may previously have overlooked or neglected become more transparent. Awareness of the breathing process also forces us to live in the moment. It reminds us that the only beauty that exists in our lives is that which can be experienced in the here and now.

Keepsake

Through the awareness of breath, the source of life, you can find inner peace.

Simplify Your Life

Most of us approach life the way Sisyphus — a character in Greek mythology who spent his life pushing a big stone up a steep hill — approached it. Whenever he managed to get the stone to the top of the hill, it would slide back down and he would have to start over again. Sisyphus lived in a perpetual rut. His preoccupation with getting the stone up the hill overshadowed his entire existence.

Life does not have to be complicated. If the daily rituals of living have become an uphill climb, take measures to simplify your life. Simplicity is an essential path all of us must take to restore order and balance in our lives. Too much clutter clouds our thought process and distracts us from our real purpose. Simplicity, on the other hand, provides us the clarity, serenity and mental strength we need to meet everyday challenges. It gives us space to get in touch with our creativity and to connect with life forces beyond and greater than ourselves.

Simplifying our lives is not a simple process. It requires sacrifice, courage and a commitment to let go of our mental and physical attachments, some of which we have spent a lifetime developing.

One of the first steps toward simplicity is to take inventory of your life. Make a checklist of everything that is weighing you down and preventing your happiness. Are you involved in relationships that are emotionally exhausting, draining you of time and energy? Are you overwhelmed by the demands of your family or friends? Are you living beyond your means to impress others? Are your social obligations burdensome? Are you carrying heavy loads of baggage from the past? Are you bogged down with material possessions that no longer serve a meaningful or functional purpose? Has your job become too demanding, limiting the time you have for yourself or your family? Answers to these types of questions can reveal what has complicated our lives and robbed us of peace and tranquility.

After taking an honest inventory of where you are, clean house. Consider what you can do to simplify your life. In some cases, this may require drastic measures. You may need to end toxic relationships that keep you on an emotional rollercoaster or to pay off your credit card debt so that bill collectors will stop nagging you. If your work has become too mundane or unfulfilling, you may want to explore new career options. I suggest that you go through every room of your house and get rid of everything that is not functional or aesthetically pleasing. Finding the path that God has chosen for us is easier when we are free of unnecessary clutter and confusion.

Not only do we have to simplify the external areas of our lives — our physical surroundings, social and intimate relationships, careers and finances — but we have to simplify our internal lives, as well. Just as we clean our homes, we have to scrub the clutter from our minds. Cleansing the mind can occur through a variety of ways: conscious breathing, gardening, silence, meditation or prayer. A mind that is filled with distrust, worry, guilt, self-doubt or regrets from the past can be as disconcerting as a messy room. It is much easier to make our hopes, dreams and aspirations known to the universe when our thinking is free and clear. By simplifying both our outer and inner lives, we make room for more blessings to flow our way.

Keepsake

Simplicity is living in the moment. Simplicity is letting go. Simplicity is embracing the truth. Simplicity is being who you are meant to be. By embracing a life of simplicity, you are able to move closer to your God-chosen path.

Live to Laugh

You repossess your life when you laugh at
the things that try you.

— Toni Morrison

Laughter is a pure form of communication. It crosses cultural boundaries. Regardless of our native language, ethnicity, creed or color, laughter is a universal response, understood and appreciated by all people around the globe. When was the last time you had a bellyaching, sidesplitting laugh? Laughter is the perfect antidote for lifting our spirits and nourishing our souls. It infuses life with joy and enthusiasm. There is nothing like a good, hearty laugh to help us experience the fullness of life.

Many of us take life and ourselves too seriously. We focus on careers, relationships, finances, physical appearance, household duties and other aspects of our lives that prevent laughter and good cheer from entering our hearts. One of the best ways to loosen our grip on life is through laughter. A good source of humor is the ability to laugh at oneself. When we are able to laugh at our own shortcomings and imperfections, we more readily empathize with the shortcomings and imperfections of others. Laughter helps us to bridge the gap between ourselves and the outside world. By taking attention away from our own problems and concerns, laughter allows us to be absorbed in something other than ourselves; it allows us to look at life in a more delightful way.

The average child laughs about a hundred times a day. The average adult laughs about twelve times a day. Like children, adults need to learn to embrace the lighter side of life. A quick-fix solution is spontaneous and frequent laughter. Laughter and good humor can transform almost any situation into a cheerful moment.

Laughter is contagious. If you see or hear someone laughing, his delight has the ability to make you laugh, even when you do not know what gave him joy. Whenever I speak with my aunt, who lives in Arkansas, our first response to recognizing each other's voice is to burst into laughter. This is our way of embracing each other across the distance and setting the tone for what we expect to be a warm and cheerful conversation. Laughter brings amusement and joyfulness to every heart it touches.

In addition to transforming and altering our state of mind, a dose of laughter also promotes good health. Scientific studies have shown that laughter stimulates our immune system, increases our energy level, lowers stress, reduces pain and provides mental clarity. According to the poet Langston Hughes, laughter is our "own unconscious therapy." It heals our wounds, keeps our lives in balance, restores our health and makes it possible for us to rise when we fall. Starting today, make it a habit to laugh as often and as much as possible. A life filled with laughter is a whole and well-balanced life.

Keepsake

Laughter is the gift of God. Laugh as much and as often as you can.

Choose Your Battles

Things which matter most must never be at the mercy of things which matter least.

— Johann Goethe

Someone cuts in line ahead of you at the grocery store. Your date arrives fifteen minutes late. The neighbor's tree branches extend onto your property. A stranger bumps into you in a crowded space. Is it really *that big a deal*? Is it necessary to get bent out of shape every time we feel violated or annoyed? In any situation we encounter, we can choose a path of conflict or a path of peace.

Some of the best advice I ever received came from my former neighbor, Miss Alberta, who lived to be 100 years old. She was as wise as time. As a child, I spent many hours on Miss Alberta's front porch, talking to her as she rocked in her chair and chewed tobacco. I recall

ROD TERRY

Miss Alberta confiding in me during one of my visits that she knew which one of the neighborhood children was stealing apples from her tree in the backyard. She mentioned that she had observed the culprit from her kitchen window twice in one week. Rather than confront him, as I suggested, she advised, "It is wiser to *choose your battles*."

By *choosing your battles*, you can make a big deal out of something, or you can let it go. This lesson applies to most situations in life. Every disagreement or misunderstanding we have with another person does not warrant a confrontation. Rather than get involved in a senseless debate over who is right or wrong, it is usually better to shrug it off. The ability to let go of a menacing encounter always provides a bridge to higher ground.

Every day, we face the possibility of a challenge that tests our resolve. To keep peace and tranquility, we have to learn to distinguish between when we should defend ourselves, and when it makes sense to back away. Addressing every perceived slight is unnecessary, especially when the stakes are low. In *Maximize the Moment*, T. D. Jakes advises, "Never go to war where there are no spoils." Confronting others in situations where the outcome will not seriously affect our well-being wastes our time and depletes our inner resources. What really matters is that we keep enough energy and strength at our disposal to protect ourselves in situations that compromise our spiritual growth and development. When we are careful about the battles we choose, we become conduits of peace and serenity.

Keepsake

In every situation you encounter, you can choose a path of peace or a path of conflict. Choose peace.

Surround Yourself
with Beauty

We should always strive to make the spaces in our lives as beautiful as possible. Just as it is important to surround ourselves with positive and nurturing people, it is equally important to surround ourselves with objects that are stimulating and aesthetically pleasing. Everything we place around us reflects our inner being. Beautiful sights, sounds, words and objects awaken our senses, nourish our soul and inspire us to dream.

Our environment shapes the way we think, feel and act. It reflects who we are and who we are striving to become. The artwork hanging on our walls, the books in our libraries, the rugs on our floors, the flowers in our gardens and even our cooking utensils are reflections of who we are. "We shape our dwellings, and afterwards our dwellings shape us," observed Winston Churchill.

When I purchased my first home, I promised myself that not only would everything I brought there be useful, but it would also appeal to my personal sense of style and beauty. I applied this standard to all my household acquisitions: furniture, appliances, cookware, bed linen, kitchen utensils and glassware. I wanted every square foot of my home to be a source of beauty and inspiration. The result has been a collection of graceful and eclectic objects in my home, which have created a sense of warmth, well-being and comfort. On my living room wall hangs a black-and-white photograph of a young boy kicking up his heels. My heart sings with joy and wonder every time I pass it, reminding me of the tenderness and innocence of life. In another room sits a wooden bowl carved from a coconut tree in Senegal; whenever I touch its round, smooth surface, it steals my breath away in amazement. My library houses hundreds of books, of different textures, sizes and shapes, whose pages inspire and uplift me.

The impact that art and objects of beauty can have on our psyche is astonishing. The slow absorption of beauty re-invigorates the soul and revives the spirit. The poet, Johann Goethe, believed, "A man should hear a little music, read a little poetry and see a fine picture every day of his life, in order that worldly fears may not obliterate the sense of the beautiful which God has implanted in the human soul."

Creating an environment of beauty does not require an interior decorator or a big budget. All you need is your imagination and creativity. We can do numerous things to enhance our environment and add beauty to our lives. Place scented candles throughout your home, using a different scent in each room to create different aromas and moods. Decorate your walls with photographs and paintings. Play soothing music. Arrange fresh flowers in your favorite vase. Cover old tables and chairs with richly textured fabrics. The range of things we can do to beautify our living space is endless. By infusing our surroundings with objects of beauty and pleasure, we can transform our environment into a living affirmation of what we want to create in our lives. The more beauty we are able to see and perceive in our lives, the more beautifully our lives will unfold.

Keepsake

Consider the things you can do to enhance your environment right now. If you only light a candle, you will be charmed by the flickering of the flame.

The Gift of Silence

A day well lived must know the shape of silence.
— Kent Nerburn

The clamor and distractions of modern living are overwhelming. We are inundated with blaring sounds that diminish our peace and tranquility. Our environments are cluttered with the cacophony of life: ringing telephones, loud music, loud people, honking horns, the hustle and bustle of the workplace, bad news pouring out of televisions and radios and the constant drone and invasiveness of cell phone chatter. No wonder it is difficult to focus on our real purpose! We are overwhelmed with all kinds of external confusion and chaos.

In order to live a more serene and peaceful life, we have to reduce the external and internal noise levels. We all need quiet time to reflect and meditate. Silence allows us to explore the deepest dimensions of our being, enabling us to hear who we really are. According to the poet, Maya Angelou, silence is an optimum state: "In silence, we listen to ourselves. Then we ask questions of ourselves. We describe ourselves to ourselves. In quietude we may even hear the voice of God."

Silence provides an inner sanctuary. It is a place where we can retreat from the overbearing influences of the outside world and be alone in the comfort of our thoughts, perceptions and feelings. When we are in a state of silence, we are able to hear things clearly that may have been muffled. We are able to enter doors of understanding that were previously closed. Out of silence come reflection, clarity, creativity, inspiration, hope and strength. During moments of quiet, we become our own purveyors of insight and enlightenment. Truth, wisdom and understanding whisper to us from within. The Book of Isaiah states, "In quietness and in confidence shall be strength."

From silence, we can move in any direction. We can confront an abusive and disrespectful spouse. We can forgive and accept ourselves. We can change jobs or careers. With confidence, we can say no to things that do not appeal to us. The power of silence is transformative. It emboldens us to explore possibilities, choices and options we never knew existed. It draws us to our truest selves.

Most of us associate silence with being in a cabin in the woods (Thoreau's *Walden* comes to mind), being alone on a deserted island, or being in the chapel of a church. However, silence emanates from within us. To experience inner calm, it is not necessary to be in a physically quiet environment. Silence can be achieved anywhere, in any situation, at any time. It is not merely the absence of noise, but a stillness of the mind, body and spirit. Once you are able to achieve silence, you can revisit it in your heart anytime, wherever you are.

In a most unusual way, I made a remarkable discovery about how silence increases awareness and mindfulness. After my stereo was stolen from my car five different times, I decided not to replace it. I had had enough. It took me a while to get accustomed to driving around town without a radio. For me, driving a car and listening to music were simultaneous acts. Still, buying another stereo was unthinkable. Surprisingly, the silence created by the lack of a stereo was empowering. It awakened me to my surroundings and gave me an opportunity to commune with myself. I learned to be at ease in my own presence and listen to my own thoughts without the distraction of music.

I have since traded in my old car for a more reliable vehicle. Although I now have a stereo, I prefer not to listen to it while I am driving. Instead, I use driving as a quiet time to pray, to think, to reflect and to solve problems. This newfound solitude helps me focus on the true meaning of life and makes me more conscious of my unique place in the universe.

Another effective way I experience silence is through meditation. To gain complete knowledge and understanding about who you are, I encourage you to spend time each day in meditation. Through silent meditation, we are able to transcend the material world and gain access to our inner source. There are many ways to meditate, but I use a simple technique. Every morning, immediately after I wake up, I set my timer for twenty minutes. I close my eyes and monitor my breathing, while repeating the mantra, "My strength is my truth. My truth is my strength." The meditation technique you use is your choice. What matters is that you meditate. I have learned that meditation clears my mind of all resistance and connects me to my inner being, allowing me to develop a deeper sense of who I am. Try to adopt meditation as a daily ritual and see how your life changes.

To connect with the essence of who we are, every soul requires silent communion. Silence is our most sacred dwelling place. It provides a solid foundation upon which we can balance our lives. More importantly, it helps us absorb what it means to be alive here and now. Give yourself the gift of silence.

Keepsake

When you find yourself at the crossroads of life, have the courage to wait in silence. The answer will come.

Eliminate Worry

Worry does not empty tomorrow of its sorrow,
it empties today of its strength.

— Corrie ten Boom

Some of our lives are consumed with worry. We have become "worry-holics." Fortunately, the things we worry about rarely happen; the bottom never falls out quite the way we imagine it will. Still, worry is a common thread of our existence. We worry about not having enough money to pay bills on time. We worry about our jobs, our health, our aging parents, our future, our children's future and our appearance. We even worry about things that are beyond our control, such as the weather and what others think about us.

Worry is a feeling of uneasiness that troubles and drains us. It projects into our future what might or could happen. It generally arises from an overactive imagination that distorts a situation and blows it way out of proportion. Worry stems from fear — not the type of fear a person feels when he is in immediate physical danger, but a psychological feeling that something bad might happen. Ironically, our most stubborn fears are usually more imagined than real. According to a Swedish proverb, worry gives a small thing a big shadow. It causes us to project a situation to its worst possible conclusion.

Worry is self-destructive. It depletes our inner resources, distorts our thoughts, drains our energy, obscures our judgment and compromises our spiritual well-being. Worry has physical effects, too; it is possible to worry oneself sick. Medical studies have shown that worry is the most common cause of sickness in human beings. Worry affects blood circulation, the glands and the nervous system. Worry can lead to depression, stomach ulcers, high blood pressure, nervous breakdowns, premature graying of hair and an array of other physical disorders.

The worst thing about worry is that it does not provide anything of value in return. Regardless of how much time and energy we spend worrying about a situation, it does nothing to improve the situation. It cannot pay a bill, influence a verdict, save a job, repair a relationship, change the weather or improve our health. Worry merely causes us to get worked up about the possibility of something bad happening in the future. The French essayist, Montaigne, wrote, "My life has been filled with terrible misfortunes, most of which never materialized."

Worry is a future tense emotion acted out in the present, with no basis other than an overactive imagination and fear. We have the capacity to cope with the challenges of each day. It is when we project fear into our future that we become overwhelmed with worry. Next time you find yourself in a worrisome situation, close your eyes for a few minutes and become aware of your breathing. Follow your breath inward and outward. This will relax you and help you realign with the will of God.

The best antidote for worry is faith. If we are able to discipline our minds so that we operate from a position of faith rather than fear, we can overcome feelings of vulnerability and powerlessness that cause us to worry. Strong faith replaces negative thoughts of fear and doubt with positive thoughts of courage and love. Faith gives us the confidence we need to trust in divine guidance and remain true to our path.

Keepsake

Worry is a result of fear. The best way to overcome worry is to remain centered in the here and now. The things we fear could happen rarely do.

Connect with Nature

In every walk with nature,
one receives far more than he seeks.

— John Muir

Nature is the foundation of life and the root of spirituality. As spiritual beings, it is essential that we make a conscious effort to engage ourselves in activities that fuel our soul and nourish our spirit. Communion with nature is a good starting point. Whether we are bird watching, stargazing or mountain climbing, we ought to have some relationship with the energies, forces and wonders of nature. Communing with nature is a critical link to living a vital, full and creative life. All one has to do is see the beauty of a rainbow, smell the fragrance of a rose, feel the warmth of the sun, listen to the howl of the wind or taste the sweetness of honeysuckle to know that nature is a source of abundance. Whenever we take time to commune with nature, we discover the presence of a power greater than ourselves.

The forces of nature are omnipresent — they exist wherever we are. There are many ways to experience the miracles and mysteries of nature, especially when we approach them with conscious intent. A brilliant sunset or a whiff of lavender in the air can be a transforming experience if we are willing to embrace our kinship with nature.

Every year, my friend Janet goes on a silent retreat in the mountains. Her favorite activity is walking through the woods along the prayer path. "While alone in the woods, I am able to connect with the trees, plants, animals and stars," she revealed to me. According to Janet, being isolated in the presence of nature is a powerful, transformative experience that makes her feel closer to God. "Each year I leave the retreat with a better understanding of who I am and my unique place in the world."

One of my favorite pastimes is gardening. My flirtation with nature usually takes place on bended knees in my front yard. My garden is a source of beauty and pleasure, which I use to create a sense of serenity and balance in my life. While cultivating my garden of red tulips, geraniums and hostas, I experience peace and tranquility. Gardening is more than digging, planting, watering and weeding. It is a spiritual journey that connects me to the natural order of the universe. Not only has my romance with gardening put me in touch with the wonders of nature, but it has also helped me to cultivate my own inner landscape. Like any affair of the heart, gardening has given my life a sense of wholeness and richness. Whether I am gardening, horseback riding or walking in the rain, I find that the real beauty of nature is that it provides a sacred space for joy, peace, love and truth to enter the fiber of our lives.

The rhythms and symbols of nature are all around us. There are magnificent places like Niagara Falls and the Grand Canyon, which are awe-inspiring. But our communion with nature does not have to be on this scale. Connecting with nature can be as simple as peeling an orange, tossing a pebble into a lake and watching the ripples appear in the water, or enjoying a fresh breeze. By communing with nature, we develop a better sense of ourselves and join forces with the flow of the universe. The restorative and healing powers of nature provide the sustenance we need to understand that our lives are an integral part of the greater whole.

Keepsake

Communing with nature can be a powerful source of inspiration. Trust nature to help you develop your natural instincts and discover your inner wisdom.

Learn to Let Go

Regardless of how hard we try, it is impossible to control every detail of our lives. It is even more difficult to control the lives of others. Trying to control people or situations only results in frustration and disappointment. In fact, most things that occur in life are beyond our control. We cannot control how others feel about us. We cannot control our body structure. We cannot control the actions of our family, friends or lovers. Therefore, nothing is more critical to preserving peace of mind than being able to let go.

For most of us, letting go is a gigantic step. Even when it is in our best interest to do so, our resistance can be difficult to overcome. We tend to define ourselves by our attachments. Our lives generally revolve around our children, our relationships, our careers, our material possessions and numerous other attachments, to which we cling. But occasionally there comes a time when we have to pull away from our attachments and let them drift away like balloons. Instead of trying to fix a broken relationship, we have to develop the strength to let go. Sometimes loving someone requires setting him free. Instead of trying to control the lives of our children, we have to give them space to make choices and experience consequences. It is not easy to surrender the things that we believe define who we are. Still, inner peace and happiness depend on our ability to let go.

Letting go is not limited to people and relationships. A good practice is to detach ourselves from all negative thoughts, fears and beliefs that compromise our peace and tranquility. We have to let go of our past. The only thing constructive about the past is learning from past lessons. It is counterproductive to hold on to bygone experiences or circumstances, making them permanent fixtures in our lives. The land of "could-have-been" is a good place to visit, but not to dwell. Life is lived in the present, not the past.

We have to let go of the notion that the type of work we do defines who we are. We are greater than our jobs or careers. In the totality of life, work is a small component of the bigger picture. We have to let go of trying to please and impress others. Our self-worth is not determined by where we live, what we wear and how we look. We also have to let go of our insatiable desire to judge and compare ourselves to others. Ultimately, it is surrendering our attachments that frees us to express our unique talents and creativity. The moment we surrender, we increase our possibility for happiness and our ability to impact humanity in a meaningful way.

The process of letting go begins with a clear understanding of one principle: everything we need is within us. There is no reason to look outside of ourselves for what we already have inside. Once we understand that, we can let everything we have been clinging to drift away, strings and all. It is only after we realize our own self-sufficiency that we can declare our independence from people, possessions and emotional situations that drain our energy and cause us to suffer. A critical part of being able to let go is having faith that God will lead us down a more peaceful path.

Keepsake

Approach life from a state of surrender. By giving up your stake in the world, you can live a more balanced and peaceful life.

Take a Day Away

*It is not in doing but in being, it is not in trying
but in trusting, it is not in rushing but in resting,
that we find the strength of God.*

— Unknown

Every morning, the race begins with the sound of the alarm clock. As soon as we awake, the demands of work, the needs of our families and the relentless desires of others overtake our lives. We must make appointments, punch clocks, meet deadlines, return calls, attend meetings, prepare meals and fulfill other obligations. Our responsibilities and commitments can consume our day, providing us with very little time for ourselves.

Because our culture places such a strong emphasis on work and productivity, most of us do not know what it means to take a break and relax. Our motors are constantly running. A sense of haste and preoccupation always surrounds us. We rush from one task to the next, ignoring the flashing yellow lights in our subconscious mind, which caution us to slow down. Doing nothing or just *being* overwhelms us with guilt. We are afraid that our idleness will corrupt us.

I agree that a strong work ethic is an admirable and necessary part of life. Most of us have to work to support ourselves and our families. But should work be the primary focus of our existence? I believe it is just as important to set aside time from our busy schedules to rest and relax. Occasionally, we need time to clear our minds and recharge our batteries. Moments of rest and relaxation give us a chance to reflect, to examine where we are and where we are going, to heal, unwind, daydream or just do nothing. In an essay, *Take a Day Away,* the poet, Maya Angelou, writes, "Each person deserves a day away in which no problems are confronted, no solutions searched for. Each of us needs to withdraw from the cares that will not withdraw from us. We need hours of aimless wandering or spates of time sitting on park benches, observing the mysterious world of ants and the canopy of treetops." Regardless of our job, our position or our endless list of things to do, we all need private time when we separate ourselves from our responsibilities. Life does not require that we always be engaged in some activity. To get the greatest benefit, we have to learn to strike a crucial balance between work and play.

Sometimes just *being* is more productive than *doing*. It is during the state of *being* that we renew our spirit and refresh our soul.

Taking a day away gives us an opportunity to refill our own vessel. It allows us to take time from our hectic pace to indulge ourselves. We owe it to ourselves occasionally to abandon our daily ritual of awakening to the sound of the alarm, rushing to get dressed for work and racing to the office. What if we were to set aside one day for ourselves every week? I know this would be a revolutionary act for most of us, but it is worth considering. Instead of going to work or attending to household duties, *take a day away*: go to the beach, drive through the park, write a poem, watch the sunset, read a novel, go window shopping or do whatever else your heart desires.

Life is too short to spend it trying to meet the never-ending demands of others. Give yourself permission to abandon the constant grind of work, and take time to savor the beauty of life. Treat yourself to a day away.

Keepsake

Schedule a date with yourself once a week and follow your bliss wherever it leads.

PART FOUR

Passionate Pursuits

~

*The only acts worth pursuing in life are those
inspired by the passion of the heart
and the longing of the soul.*

Move Out of
Your Comfort Zone

We are creatures of habit. Much of what we do each day is a matter of routine. We work the same job for years; we reside in the same community or neighborhood where we grew up; we eat at the same restaurants; we socialize with the same group of people or we take the same route to work every day. Our overall approach to life rarely changes. Instead of being creative, and allowing ourselves to explore new ideas and adventures, we cling to the familiar. Living within a comfort zone of familiarity and routine makes us feel safe, even though our sense of security is an illusion.

At the core of living in a comfort zone is fear. Fear is like a puppeteer that pulls our strings and keeps us from doing what we are capable of doing. For many, undertaking a new challenge or following an unbeaten path is a daunting experience. We are afraid that we are not worthy or good enough. What if I fail? What if I do not measure up? What if I do not like the food? What if I get lost? What if I am not smart enough? What if I do not fit in? These questions of self-doubt linger in our minds when we are faced with possibilities for change. Even if it is doing something as simple as trying a new restaurant or taking a different route to work, the risk of trying something diverse seems too much for us to bear. Still, we can start today to transcend our fears.

How do we transcend fear and the illusion of comfort? We can move beyond our comfort zone by believing in our talents and abilities, by being open and receptive to possibilities for change or by trusting the universe to guide us.

Life is a process of growth and change. To grow and evolve into the best persons we can be, we must have the courage and the faith to take chances. Risk-taking is a fundamental part of living a meaningful life. We cannot spend our entire lives fishing from the same pond. By forcing ourselves to break free of our ordinary routines, we are able to experience the boundless.

As creatures of nature, our divine mission is to flourish and grow. Flowers do not avoid blooming because of the risk of frost; they bloom because it is the nature of being a flower. Fireflies do not refrain from flashing their light because they risk being detected; they light because it is the nature of being a firefly. Like other creatures of nature, our purpose on earth is to live up to our fullest potential; this is the nature of being human. To manifest the best of life, we must dare to live.

Despite our fear of moving beyond our comfort zone, we have to trust that the actions we take are in divine order. Even in apparent failure, we learn and grow. We do not honor our Creator or ourselves when we avoid opportunities for growth. As Helen Keller profoundly noted, "Life is either a daring adventure or nothing."

Keepsake

You are unlimited. Learn to live outside of your comfort zone by embracing new and unexplored paths.

Find Work You Love

Nothing steals the joy from life like an unfulfilling job. Work dominates most of our lives. A large amount of our time each day is spent working, preparing for work or traveling to and from work. As a result, the type of work we do is a vital part of our happiness and spiritual well-being. In order to live a balanced and purposeful life, it is important that we choose satisfying and meaningful work.

I mentioned in an earlier chapter that after graduating from law school, I got a job as an associate with a firm in Pittsburgh. I earned an impressive salary and received excellent health and retirement benefits. I had a nice office with a panoramic view of the Allegheny River, my own secretary, an expense account and plenty of other perks. I could not have dreamed of a more ideal situation. However, within a few months of working at the firm, my enthusiasm for the job began to dissipate. Instead of dealing with substantive issues of corporate law and finance as I expected, I spent most of my work-day doing first-year associate grunt work and balancing a tightrope of office politics and gossip.

While my family and friends reveled in what they perceived to be my success, I was falling apart on the inside. Some days, I would leave work, drive home and fall across the bed in my clothes. After almost two grueling years of boring job assignments and an unfriendly work environment, I found the courage to resign. "Take this job and shove it" was playing in my mind as I wrote my letter of resignation. Instantly, I felt the heavy burden I had been carrying lift from my body. I felt lighter, and the wrinkles smoothed from my brow. I had freed myself from the drudgery of a loath-some job. That experience taught me a valuable lesson: Finding work that you love is a fundamental aspect of life. It is a sad reality that many of us never experi-ence gratifying work. Rarely do we stop to consider whether the type of work we do is consistent with our real purpose in life. Most of us view work as a financial means to an end. We are motivated by getting instead of giving. As someone who held a string of uninspiring jobs just to get paid, I know what it feels like to be on a precipitous course to nowhere.

Our attitude toward work, however, is not entirely our fault. It is based on a cultural work ethic that promotes work as a duty performed out of necessity, rather than an opportunity for creative and passionate pursuits. Clearly, there is more to work than earning a paycheck. Through our work, we are able to express ourselves and make a positive difference in the world. When we commit to fulfilling and rewarding work that satisfies our need to be creative and also serves the good of humanity, we infuse our lives with meaning and purpose.

The quest to find work that we love is no small task. Discovering our creative passion requires us to spend some time alone, without the interruptions and influences of those around us. We must constantly ask ourselves, *What have I been put on earth to do with my life? What is my purpose?* These are bold and courageous questions that require serious introspection. Only after we have embraced and contemplated these questions in a heartfelt and meaningful way can we find our true calling.

Today, during a quiet moment, ask yourself what your passion is, and seriously consider how you can make a living doing it. The moment you begin to take steps in that direction, you will feel great satisfaction and discover a new world of opportunity.

Keepsake

Your life is much more significant than the way you earn a living. You are created in the image of God. You have been put on Earth to fulfill the promises of the universe.

Do Your Best

A good approach to living a fulfilling and purposeful life is to make the best use of our God-given resources. All of us are endowed with enormous potential; we have an amazing capacity to build, evolve, create and grow. Still, many of us choose to build our lives around images and illusions that are impossible to sustain. Instead of loving and accepting ourselves as we are, we strive for perfection. We want the perfect face and body, the perfect job, the perfect house, the perfect spouse and the perfect family. Nothing is perfect. Any quest for perfection is futile. It is like burning wood without fire. Rather than trying to achieve such unrealistic goals, we should strive simply to *do our best*.

Doing our best is a self-contained principle, which can only be measured by personal standards. Doing our best means using all our talents and abilities to the fullest potential, being able to recognize our weaknesses and maximize our strengths, and living up to our own standards. In any situation, as long as we do our best, we never have to worry about the result of our efforts. It is only when we do less than our best that we subject ourselves to self-doubt, judgment and regret.

Doing our best, however, does not always guarantee success, especially when measured by external standards. Regardless of our efforts, not every picture we paint will be a masterpiece, nor will we earn a promotion at every job. Sometimes it is necessary to fail in order to know our true strengths. Even in situations where we fail or fall short of our expectations, we can walk away with our heads held high when we know that we have given our best effort.

Perhaps the greatest guidance can be found in the words of Dr. Martin Luther King, Jr.: "If it falls on your lot to be a street-sweeper, sweep streets as Beethoven composed music, sweep streets as Shakespeare wrote poetry. Sweep streets so well that all the host of heaven and earth will have to pause and say, here lived a great street sweeper who swept his job well." In the final analysis of life, it is not what we do that matters; rather, it is how we do it.

Keepsake

Doing your best means living from your heart and soul. It is relying on and trusting your talents and abilities to get the job done. What others say or think about you is of no consequence when you know you have achieved your personal best.

Set Goals

One of the basic strategies for succeeding in life is to set goals. Goals challenge and inspire us to be better than we are. They stretch and enlarge the depth of our potential in ways unimaginable. Without goals to guide and direct us, we are lost. Goals focus our attention, invigorate our spirits and make it possible to live fruitful and purposeful lives. They provide us with a clear understanding of what we want out of life and a viable framework for making it happen. Although it may seem easier to take life as it comes, life is simpler and more meaningful when we set goals and have a mission.

Setting goals and achieving them is no small matter. The accomplishment of goals requires serious commitment, self-discipline and pragmatism. We must be prepared to make enormous sacrifices and allow ourselves to be guided by abiding faith. Once we commit to reaching our goals, however, Providence moves in our favor, and all the forces of the universe are brought to bear to assist and support us.

It is important that the goals we set for ourselves are not so vague or intangible that we are unable to define a clear plan for bringing them to fruition. Goals should be specific and concrete. For example, if your goal is to obtain a college degree, decide where you would like to attend college and determine what area of study you would like to pursue. If your goal is to lose weight, determine exactly how many pounds you would like to lose and devise a plan to achieve your goal. If your goal is to purchase a new house, make a list of the locations where you would like to live and determine your price range. If you have a desire to earn a specific salary, write down the amount you would like to make before you begin your job search. The more specific our goals, the more attainable they become.

It is also important that the breadth and scope of the goals we set for ourselves be within reason. Goals are more attainable when they are driven by a strong desire to achieve self-actualization. These types of goals push us to our limits intellectually, creatively, physically and spiritually.

One of the first steps toward achieving our goals is writing them down. The act of writing our goals converts them from mere thoughts to plans of action. They become permanently etched in our psyche, increasing their chance of realization. It is much easier to accomplish specific goals than to actualize transient thoughts that merely exist in our minds.

The types of goals we set for ourselves are personal choices. One might set a short-term goal to visit a museum, paint a room or learn a prayer. A long-term goal may include starting a family or writing a book. As long as it is realistic, the nature or extent of the goal is irrelevant. It is the step-by-step process of achieving a goal that enriches and transforms us.

We are all responsible for the shape and course of our lives. It is bad judgment to assume that life will take care of itself or to place our destiny in the hands of someone else. One way to achieve success is to set goals and pursue them with great resolve. As long as we keep moving forward, the attainment of any goal is possible.

Keepsake

Goals keep you aligned with your purpose. Pursuing your purpose and reaching your goals are parts of the same journey.

Approach Life with Enthusiasm

My friends tell me it does not take much to excite me. I agree with them. I have a natural exuberance for life. Life fascinates me: the changing seasons; an unexpected call from an old friend; the first taste of a scrumptious meal; crawling between fresh sheets; wearing a new pair of shoes; driving across the Chesapeake Bay Bridge; being awakened in the morning by birds singing at my window. I embrace life — even the mundane and ordinary aspects — with passion and enthusiasm.

I attribute my sense of enthusiasm to a passage I read many years ago, scribbled on the wall of a building: "Always be enthusiastic about life and everything you do." That message changed my outlook on life. I took it to heart as though it had been written exclusively for me. It became my mantra for living. Inspired by the passage, I went from being a low-key, take-life-in-stride type of guy to a consummate enthusiast.

Enthusiasm for life is the best gift we can give to ourselves. When we are enthusiastic, we live our lives as an expression of pure spirit. Enthusiasm infuses us with excitement and joy. It enables us to live richer, more vibrant and more abundant lives. Passion for life inspires, uplifts and motivates us to thrive. Living without enthusiasm is like trying to learn a new dance without feeling the beat of the music. Our passion for living can be detected by the twinkle in our eyes, the swing in our gait, the glow in our face or the pitch of our voice. These are outward expressions that convey to the world that we feel good about what we are doing and about ourselves. Others appreciate being around us when we show appreciation for life.

It is unlikely that I will forget Cuba Gooding, Jr.'s heartfelt expression of enthusiasm when he won an Oscar several years ago for his role in the movie, *Jerry Macguire*. In an overwhelming display of emotion and excitement, Gooding brought down the house while delivering his acceptance speech. Although the Academy Awards is usually a carefully staged event, Gooding's upbeat presence electrified the audience and garnered him a standing ovation. I am sure his passion captured the attention and the hearts of people around the world.

Had Gooding not been so passionate about receiving the Oscar, he would have faded into the background like the many other actors who accepted their awards. As the audience's reaction to Cuba Gooding demonstrated, enthusiasm is contagious. To transcend the normalcy of life we must have a zest for living. Enthusiasm is a magnetic and powerful force that we should dare to make a part of our everyday lives.

When we approach life with passion and enthusiasm, we expose hidden dimensions of our lives that allow us to connect with others in a more meaningful way. The energy that enthusiasm creates allows us to experience the fullness of life. Follow your passion!

Keepsake

Be the most enthusiastic person you know. When you are enthusiastic about life, you express every aspect of who you are.

If Not Now, When?

O ne of the privileges of being human is the ability to do as we please. Unlike other species that rely on their natural instincts for survival, we have the capacity to make decisions and choices about how we live. We are willful beings. Most of the steps we take in life are deliberate and intentional. We are the masters of our destiny. If we have the will, we can create, build or accomplish anything we desire.

One thing that undermines human potential more than anything else is procrastination. Procrastination is a self-defeating behavior that causes us to put off until tomorrow the things that ought to be done today. It compromises our hopes, dreams and aspirations. Instead of taking action and doing what needs to be done, procrastination causes us to squander our resources by doing nothing, even when we know that the consequences can hurt us.

It can be dangerous and unhealthy for us to procrastinate. Procrastinating can compromise our self-respect, lower our self-esteem and jeopardize our relationships, careers, finances and health. One of the keys to living a fulfilling and exciting life, maintaining a successful career and feeling good about ourselves is to develop the ability to start and complete important projects. Otherwise, we become victims of procrastination, and thus sabotage our future.

An example of procrastination is putting off filing income tax returns until the last minute. Although we are fully aware that filing late can result in penalties ranging from interest and fees to criminal prosecution, we still fail to file in a timely manner. An even more serious example of procrastination is avoiding going to the doctor when we have symptoms of ill health. Physical symptoms, such as a strange lump or shortness of breath, suggest a need for immediate medical attention, yet we delay seeking a diagnosis and treatment. Obviously, whenever we respond to serious health concerns in a dilatory manner, the prognosis can be much worse than it would have been had we sought medical attention sooner. Another example of procrastination is staying in a bad relationship with the hope that it will improve with time. Although we know the relationship cannot be salvaged, we remain in it, delaying the inevitable. These situations represent procrastination at its worst. They paint a clear picture of how it can undermine our potential.

The way to overcome procrastination is to take immediate action. Often, too much contemplation or waiting for the right time can be counterproductive. The present is always ripe for meaningful and positive change. Right now, what are you putting off? What goal or project are you delaying? If there is anything in life you wish to accomplish, now is the perfect time to pursue your dreams. Whether buying a house, writing a book, losing weight, starting your own business, earning a college degree or ending an unhealthy relationship, once you take the initial step towards reaching your goal, the universal tides of support will rise and meet you. A powerful question we should constantly ask ourselves is, If not now, when?

Keepsake

The best antidote for procrastination is action. Stop waiting for the perfect time or situation; start planting seeds today for a more rewarding life.

Make Each Day Count

Every day that the sun rises is filled with hope and possibility. The secret to living a rich and full life is learning to make each day count. Each day of our lives is meant to be a celebration of love and growth, filled with adventure and new discoveries. However, what boggles the mind is how many of us are willing to leave our lives hanging in the balance while we wait for a special occasion or event to occur. Instead of living in the moment and enjoying *each* day of our lives, many of us devote all our time and energy to preparing for tomorrow. Children learn early to live their lives in anticipation of the future. My ten-year-old cousin, Blake, was so excited about the release of the book, *Harry Potter and the Deathly Hallows* by J. K. Rowling, that for three days he could not concentrate or think about anything else. Similarly, adults can hardly wait to celebrate birthdays, wedding and job anniversaries, Christmas and Valentine's Day, or other special occasions. We are so obsessed with the future that we cannot enjoy the reality of today. Ordinary days are treated like mundane occurrences that have no significance. We ignore the words of the Psalmist, "This is the day which the Lord hath made; I will rejoice and be glad in it."

Life is much more than episodic birthdays, anniversaries, holidays or major sporting events, which occur once a year. In life, *every* day counts. Try not to be so anxious about tomorrow that you fail to notice what is happening in your life today. Every day is a blessing, an opportunity to spread our wings and soar to new and unforeseen heights.

Instead of trampling over the days of the week to get to "Thank God it's Friday," or some other special occasion, slow down and learn to savor the beauty in each day. This day, here and now, is all we have. It is the total embodiment of our present existence. Tomorrow is not yet ours to claim.

Keepsake

Each day on earth is a gift from God. The best way to honor the Creator and ourselves is to make each day count. Embrace each day with passion and vigor.

Dare to Dream

The only courage you ever need
is the courage to live your own dreams.

— Oprah Winfrey

Dreams are the source of hope and possibility. They help us to see ourselves as we could be, rather than as we are. Everything ever created or achieved in the world was inspired by someone who dared to dream. Life is more meaningful when we have dreams to motivate and inspire us. When I arrived in the District of Columbia to study law, I had exactly one thousand dollars in cash, a metal trunk filled with clothing, a patchwork quilt from my grandmother, fresh memories of family and friends, who had wished me well, and a dream to become an attorney. I had clung to my dream since the sixth grade. Eventually, the money ran out. I outgrew the clothes. The quilt became frayed and tattered, and the memories of those who had wished me well began to fade. The only thing that sustained me was my dream. For many years, it was the lifeline of my existence.

Dreams are potent forces. Regardless of our present circumstances, dreams can change our lives. Many people have relied on lofty dreams of success to liberate them from adverse conditions. Take, for example, the artist, Francis Deceus, who immigrated to this country from the Republic of Côte d'Ivoire. Since boyhood, Deceus had dreamed of becoming a painter. However, pursuing his dream in Côte d'Ivoire seemed impossible. As the oldest of seven children, he was expected to help his family earn a living. Most of his time was spent harvesting cocoa and herding llamas, which was very demanding and intense work. Survival in a heavily agrarian economy required full dedication from every member of his family. There was little time for "frivolous pursuits," which was how his father characterized his interest in painting.

As quickly as the wind changes directions, so, too, can a person's fate. One day a French photojournalist filming a documentary in Côte d'Ivoire happened upon a drawing that Deceus had given to a village elder. Impressed by the boy's talent, the Frenchman sought him out. He told Deceus about the École nationale supérieure des Beaux-Arts, a famous art school in

Paris, France. Deceus was flattered by the Frenchman's admiration of his work. However, to go from herding llamas in Côte d'Ivoire to studying art at the École nationale supérieure des Beaux-Arts was a bigger feat than Deceus dared to imagine. And for years, he did not do so. He simply put it out of his mind.

A few years later, in an unexpected turn of events, Deceus had an opportunity to travel to France. The prospect of going to France changed his whole outlook on life. He suddenly began to dream about attending art school in Paris. Even his father welcomed his chance to travel to France in search of a better way of life.

As it happened, France was not the land of milk and honey that Deceus had envisioned. He spoke French because Côte d'Ivoire is a former colony of France. Still, when he arrived at Montmartre, he had little money, no family and little hope. He did have his talent and his dream to paint. To make ends meet, he painted pictures and sold them on the street. After living on the income from street sales for almost a year, Deceus's talent was recognized by the owner of a local gallery, Raoul Gauthier. Gauthier, a man of great wealth and influence, took Deceus under his wing. He treated him like a surrogate brother. Using his contacts in the art world, Gauthier set in motion a chain of events, which included Deceus's enrollment in the École nationale supérieure des Beaux-Arts. Deceus's life changed forever.

Today, Deceus is an accomplished painter. His work hangs in museums and galleries around the world. His story demonstrates that dreams can come true. With the proper care and attention, our dreams can grow into wonderful creations.

Keepsake

Dreams are the foundation of reality. Anything that can be conceived in your mind can be brought to fruition.

Take Risks

The guy who takes a chance, who walks the line
between the known and unknown,
who is unafraid of failure, will succeed.

— Gordon Parks

Taking risks is one of the growing pains of life. A surefire way in which we can know the true strength of our character, the depth of our soul, the full weight of our thoughts or the size of our heart is by taking risks. Every risk we take is an opportunity for growth, a step toward self-discovery. Risks reveal to us a greater understanding of who we are by forcing us to exceed our usual limits. According to author Marianne Williamson, the purpose of our lives is to give birth to the best that is within us. One way to achieve this lofty goal is by taking risks.

Room for risk-taking lies in every aspect of our lives. Very little is so sacred that it cannot be changed.

Especially for love, we must be willing to reach out and take a chance. For example, if you have been admiring someone from a distance whom you would like to know better, do not be timid. Make a move. Tell him that his smile caught your attention, and ask if he would be interested in dinner later. Times have changed. Finding love sometimes requires bold measures. The worst he can do is say no. Love is worth the risk.

If you have been dreaming of quitting your nine-to-five and starting your own business, but have not found the courage to do it, the time is now. The present is always a perfect opportunity to sow new seeds. The way to discover our true calling and to achieve our personal best is by taking risks. To move forward in life, we must be willing to step outside of our comfort zone, even if it means leaving the perceived safety and security of our jobs.

Even in less important situations, like deciding what to wear, we have every right to be as daring and as risky as we choose. Do not allow prudish, conventional modes of thinking to dictate your style. If you have a brightly colored blouse or shirt hanging in the closet that you have been dying to wear, but have been reluctant to because you are not sure if it is you or you are afraid of how you will be perceived, go ahead and wear it anyway. Life is about taking chances and being able to express our creativity and individuality. It is healthy to break away from the usual modes of thinking or expectation.

The potential for expansion in our lives increases when we take risks and move outside of our zone of comfort. Although change may not come immediately, progress is inevitable. There are countless stories of intelligent, capable people who are trapped in dead-end jobs and unhealthy relationships. They have allowed themselves to become stifled because they do not have the courage to risk change. Complacency causes us to settle for less than we deserve, and it grinds away at the spirit. To reach our greatest potential, we must take chances. The rewards always outweigh the risks.

Keepsake

Without taking risks, you cannot grow and evolve. The more risks you take, the stronger and more powerful you will become.

PART FIVE

Divine
Revelations

~

Deep within each of us are fundamental spiritual
truths that illuminate our journey through life.
With a clear head, a pure heart and abiding faith,
we all have the capacity to manifest peace and
make our lives an extension of divinity.

A Testimony of Faith

Prayer is asking for rain. Faith is carrying an umbrella.
— Iyanla Vanzant

What makes a man who has nothing believe that he can have anything his heart desires? How does a woman find the strength to collect herself in the middle of the night and escape a violent and abusive relationship? Where does a child get the courage to take his first step? How do the blind find their way despite their challenge? What gives us the courage to face a new day, not knowing what lies ahead? The answer is faith.

Faith is the centerpiece of our existence. Faith gives us the confidence to live, to change, to grow, to love — to be who we are meant to be. It anchors us amid all the possibilities of life. It also provides the courage we need to face life's uncertainties. Susan Taylor, author of *In the Spirit,* defines faith as the flip side of fear. In order to have fulfilling, productive lives, we must replace fear with faith. Faith helps us overcome the feelings of lack, impatience, anger and distrust that are rooted in fear. With a strong sense of faith, we can move in any direction.

In a testimony of faith, the poet, Maya Angelou, declared, "I am able to go out of darkness into darkness because I have faith." To have faith is to believe unconditionally in a power greater than our own. It is a sense of inner knowing that God is on our side and He has a divine purpose and plan for our lives. How do we build faith? A strong sense of faith is the result of trusting that we are provided with everything we need to live fully. It is believing in our own power to love and prosper.

Every day we face circumstances that challenge our faith. Life swings back and forth like a pendulum in a clock. With a single stroke, our perception of life can swing from happiness to despair, from success to failure or from serenity to chaos. One moment, we can be on top of the world enjoying the bounty of success; and the next, in the basement of despair, bemoaning our defeat. From day to day, only God knows what path our lives will take. The best way to deal with the ebb and flow of life is to maintain an abiding sense of faith. Faith is the lone beacon of light that sustains us in moments of darkness and despair.

It was faith that guided Harriet Tubman toward the North Star. It was faith that sustained Mother Theresa in the poorhouses of Calcutta. It was faith that held the country together and gave us the strength to move forward after the September 11th terrorist attacks.

Faith empowers. Faith heals. Faith is like an invisible companion that is always present to guide us through the storms of life, liberating us from the clutches of fear and strengthening us to live in alignment with the divine will of God.

～

Keepsake

Through faith in the Divine, anything is possible. You can overcome perceived obstacles and conquer your fears.

A Hundred Blessings

If the only prayer you ever say in your life is thank you,
it will be enough.

— Meister Eckart

I read an interesting story about an ancient temple in Thailand. Located at the foot of the temple on the ground are a hundred brass bowls. When visiting the temple, it is customary to drop a coin in each bowl as you pass by. As the coin vibrates in the bowl, you are supposed to give thanks for a blessing you have received.

If you were at the foot of the temple, what hundred blessings would you acknowledge? Perhaps you would express gratitude for being alive, for being healthy, for being intelligent or for having the capacity to love and be loved. What blessings are you most grateful for at this moment? While we may never make the journey to the ancient temple in Thailand, we can count our blessings right where we are.

There are many reasons to be thankful. Blessings are all around, if only we would take time to appreciate and acknowledge them. The sunrise and a breath of fresh air are blessings that many of us take for granted. We can express gratitude for an endless array of people, material possessions and circumstances.

In everything give thanks. The ability to recognize our blessings brings balance, inner peace and meaning to our lives. Where there is gratitude, there is love. Gratitude is the highest form of praise that any of us can give. When we give praises for what we have, God blesses us with even more. According to Iyanla Vanzant, author of *Acts of Faith*, "An attitude of praise and thanksgiving activates the divine laws of abundance." By acknowledging our blessings, we send a message to God that we are receptive to His benevolence.

A central part of this lesson in gratitude is that we should not take our blessings for granted. Our journey through life is enhanced by the blessings we receive. Most of our blessings are ordinary experiences of daily life. Having an umbrella in our possession on a rainy day is as much a blessing as a safe flight in an airplane. Every blessing, whether large or small, is a gift from God. At all times, we should express gratitude and give thanks to our Creator for our many blessings.

The more we count our blessings, the richer our lives will become.

Keepsake

What you have at this moment is all you need. Live in a state of gratitude. Count your blessings and open yourself to infinite abundance.

To Forgive Is Divine

Forgiveness is vital to our well-being. It is the process of releasing blame, anger or resentment against someone who has hurt or disappointed us. The ability to forgive heals old wounds and liberates us from past burdens. By releasing the emotional debts of others, forgiveness clears the way for love, peace and understanding to enter our lives. It enables us to transcend negative feelings of hurt and vengeance that hold us back and prevent us from focusing on our real purpose.

The road to forgiveness can be a bumpy ride, especially when pain and resentment run deep; however, our happiness and peace of mind depend on it. Being able to forgive is the first step toward healing a heavy heart. It is necessary to break the cycle of resistance and blame that can overtake us and cause continuous pain.

I have a friend who, at the age of forty, is still struggling to overcome the emotional abuse and neglect she received as a child from her mother. Not a day goes by that she does not mention how her mother selfishly put her own personal needs and interests above the love and nourishment of her children. Nevertheless, until my friend is able to come to terms with her past and release the old wounds of pain and resentment she harbors toward her mother, peace will never manifest in her life. She will always be haunted by the grievances of her past.

The act of forgiveness is neither an excuse for a person's behavior, nor an invitation for someone to hurt us again. True forgiveness liberates our soul; it is necessary for self-preservation. The power to forgive gives us the strength to make amends with someone who has hurt us, so we can move on with our lives.

Genuine forgiveness does not happen by accident or with the passage of time. It is a conscious and deliberate choice, a practical realization that holding a grudge or seeking revenge against someone binds us to them. By shifting blame from others, forgiveness allows us to take responsibility for our own lives. Close your eyes for a moment and think of someone who has hurt you. Let all the anger and resentment you feel toward the person rise to the surface. Embrace the pain. Now, take a deep breath and forgive him or her. Forgiveness allows you to surrender the pain and move on, whether the wrongdoer is apologetic or not.

Not only is it necessary to forgive others, but it is also essential that we learn to forgive our own failures and shortcomings, which may have caused us to harbor feelings of self-doubt or shame. Forgiveness and acceptance of ourselves is the turning point toward self-actualization. It is also an acknowledgment that even our most painful and disappointing experiences have helped shape who we are today.

By forgiving ourselves and others, we are able to move toward wholeness and inner peace. In the final analysis, forgiveness is an act of love. It is the way to bridge the gap that keeps two people apart, making it possible for them to walk together.

Keepsake

Forgiveness is a gift you give to yourself. It allows you to find comfort when you are in pain. The healing power of forgiveness leads to greater hope and spiritual growth. Through your willingness to forgive, you can become an instrument of peace.

This Too Shall Pass

Gray skies are just clouds passing over.
— Duke Ellington

Has life thrown you a curve? Are you involved in an abusive relationship, a family dispute, a financial slump or an unfulfilling job that is stealing your joy and making your life miserable? Regardless of how hard we try to bring order and balance to our lives, conflict looms just around the corner; it is an inevitable part of life. As sure as the sky is blue and the ocean is wide, there will be temporary setbacks, disappointments, trials and obstacles that challenge us.

The good news is that our greatest insights are often shaped by our greatest challenges. Hardship and misfortune are put on our path to strengthen us, not to break us. Before we learn the lessons we need to learn, sometimes it is necessary to reach rock bottom. Recall the story of Imelda (in the chapter *Build Self-Esteem*), whose husband walked out on her after nine years of marriage. Although this experience emotionally devastated Imelda and caused her enormous pain, in the long run, her soul-searching made her a much stronger person. As a result of the divorce, Imelda was ultimately able to recognize her worth and come into her own power.

Episodes of distress and failure are often blessings in disguise. Not only do they make us stronger, but they also teach us important lessons in forgiveness, compassion, grace, humility and empathy. Once we are able to come to terms with the pain and suffering, we can move past the hurt and begin to heal. It is not an easy process, but it is possible.

Rather than feel sorry for ourselves when we encounter misfortune, we must face our troubles graciously. Otherwise, we risk becoming stuck in a mode of victimization. The wisdom and understanding we gain through adversity have great value in our lives. Processing pain can be a transcendent experience. It can help to define who we are and to examine where we are on our life's journey. Learning to process pain also can help us to grow and become more compassionate.

Regardless of how difficult we perceive our life's challenges to be, we can overcome any obstacles. God gives us more than enough strength to sustain ourselves through the trials and tribulations of life. We have the inner power to handle any crisis imaginable with steadfastness, faith and perseverance. Take a moment and look back over your life. Have you ever experienced an unpleasant situation or serious problem you have not survived? According to Susan Taylor, author of *In the Spirit*, "Our biggest problems in life come not so much from the difficulties we confront, but from how we perceive and respond to them."

There is abundant hope in life. The key to overcoming adversity is always to maintain a courageous and triumphant spirit. Rather than allowing yourself to be thrown off balance every time a new challenge arises, adopt the philosophy that *this too shall pass*.

All our troubles are temporary, regardless of how difficult they appear to be; however, the lessons they teach us are everlasting.

Keepsake

View every personal crisis as an opportunity for spiritual growth. Even the worst situation has a silver lining.

Live and Trust

On a recent trip home to Arkansas, the first leg of my flight from Washington, DC to Dallas was delayed. As a result, I had only ten minutes to catch my connecting flight. Racing through the airport with a garment bag over my left shoulder and luggage in my right hand, I accidentally bumped into a lady who was strolling about the terminal. Even though I was in a hurry, I stopped to apologize. She smiled at me and graciously accepted my apology. As I walked away, I heard her whisper, "Live and trust!" I was perplexed. What did she mean by *live and trust*? As I processed her comment more deeply, it occurred to me that she was telling me to slow down and have faith that I would catch my flight.

Inspired by the lady's advice, I took a deep breath and relaxed. Immediately, a sense of calm overtook my body. I slowed my hurried pace and composed myself. Was it necessary for me to rush through the airport, stressed out about a situation completely beyond my control? When I arrived at the gate, I had plenty of time because my connecting flight was delayed. This experience taught me that when I simply *live and trust,* everything will work out.

We learn our most important lessons through various experiences of daily life. As sure as the sun rises in the East and sets in the West, most external circumstances are beyond our control. We cannot change the rules to suit our personal needs; life has its own way of unfolding. Rather than attempting to change the reality of events and circumstances, it is more sensible to harmonize our actions with them. This simply means always being open and receptive to the flow of the universe.

A good strategy for living is to develop the ability to accept the things that cannot be changed. In situations beyond our control, like the weather, the behavior of others and even the arrival and departure of airplanes, it helps to understand that they are outside our sphere of influence and to accept them. Otherwise, we risk perpetual disappointment and frustration over situations we cannot control. Once we accept that some things are within our control and others are not, it is easier to follow the spiritual and emotional path God has laid before us.

Keepsake

You cannot control every detail of your life, but you *can* control how you respond to life's challenges. The best way to overcome setbacks and remain centered is to trust yourself.

Listen to Your Inner Voice

Throughout time, spiritual teachers of all traditions have espoused the benefit of listening to our inner voice. The inner voice is a powerful source of knowledge and wisdom buried deep within us. It is omniscient: it knows everything there is to know about human experience and the world we inhabit. It is a voice of truth and reason that connects us to a power greater than ourselves. When we listen to the guidance of our inner voice, there is no barrier we cannot overcome, no wall we cannot climb and no problem we cannot solve.

Our inner voice is a storehouse of wisdom and understanding that we can access if we are willing to listen to it. It speaks to our deepest needs and aspirations. Unlike listening to a conversation, listening to our inner voice requires a deep concentration and stillness of the mind. Only after we have calmed our minds can we access the inner workings of our souls.

Quieting the mind can be achieved by meditation, prayer, moments of silence, long walks, gardening, a drive through the park or any other contemplative action that relaxes us and slows down our thought processes. Once we reach a higher state of consciousness, we become conduits for the Higher Power of the universe to flow into our world.

Rarely does our inner voice speak to us through words. It usually comes to us in the form of images, urges, hunches or intuition. It comes as a gut feeling that something is right or wrong. It is the same feeling of knowing that one gets before making an important decision.

Although we are not always attuned to our innermost perceptions, our inner voice is always there to lead and guide us. In every situation we encounter in life — whom to befriend, where to live, where to work and even what to say — our inner voice is a reliable source of wisdom and guidance.

One of my biggest investments was purchasing my first home. While house hunting, I found two equally appealing and affordable houses on the same block. The first one had a beautiful spiral staircase and a master bedroom suite on the third floor with a magnificent view of the U.S. Capitol. The other house had a neoclassical interior with high ceilings and columns, and shutters in every window. For weeks, I agonized over which house to buy. Unable to make a decision, I prayed and listened to the guidance of my inner voice. Almost instantly, the image of the house I was to buy revealed itself to me. Although the spiral staircase appealed to me in the first house, I followed my intuition and bought the house with the high ceilings and columns.

About a year later, I met the lady who bought the first house that I had considered. I asked how she was enjoying her new home. She complained, "Getting furniture up the spiral staircase has been a nightmare." Although I sympathized with her, hearing her complain about the staircase reassured me of the power of listening to my inner voice. Because I listened, I am enjoying my home.

Life moves at a different level than what is observable on the surface. Once we are able to tap into our inner voice, our whole outlook on life changes. We are automatically impelled by our personal strengths. The universe opens doors for us that we never knew existed. It guides us in a new direction of self-discovery and actualization, which allows us to reach our greatest potential.

Keepsake

Everything you need to know about your existence comes from within you. When you have questions about your place in the world, listen to your inner voice for guidance. Like a candle in the night, our inner voice illuminates the dark corners of our lives and sheds light on the truth.

Epilogue

Build Your Own
Hope Chest

In the preceding pages, *Hope Chest* takes an old and revered tradition and uses it as a metaphor to reveal what is truly important in life. The purpose of the spiritual keepsakes in *Hope Chest* is to remind us that we are in control of our destiny, and that there is always an abundance of hope to sustain us on our journey. Although a book is a valuable resource, words on a page are not enough to nourish our spiritual growth and development. To really grow and have complete understanding of who we are, we must actively participate in our own self-discovery. We must do the inner work that is necessary to make us whole. One way to do this is to build a hope chest. Building a hope chest will help you uncover things about yourself that you never knew existed. It will help you identify what motivates you, what inspires you, and what attracts you. Ultimately, a hope chest will help you identify your true purpose in life.

So, in conjunction with reading this book, I encourage you to build a hope chest. The process of building a hope chest should be as sacred as building an altar. Not only will it connect you to the infinite wisdom of the universe, but it will also reveal to you what your soul and spirit are conspiring to create in your life. Because God gives us creative license to make choices and decide what is best for our lives, the path we should take is not always clear. Creating a hope chest will help to clarify your life's calling and attract the things in life that you desire.

The first step in building a hope chest is to choose a box with a cover. The box can be made of wood, straw, cardboard or metal, and it can be large or small. The only requirement is that it appeals to your personal sense of style and taste. After selecting a box, the next and most important step is deciding what to put in it. Be careful and thoughtful about the items you put in your hope chest. These items will direct you to your destiny and keep you focused on your spiritual journey through life. It is essential that everything that goes into your hope chest reflect your needs, dreams, goals, hopes and desires. Only those things that personify who you are, or who you are striving to become, should be placed in your hope chest. Although the items you select are a matter of personal choice, I recommend keepsakes that empower, strengthen and enrich your daily life. Such items may include affirmations, favorite quotations, poetry, newspaper and magazine articles, greeting cards, books, photographs, love letters, journals or any other items that motivate or inspire you to discover who you are. Self-discovery is the key to true happiness and inner peace.

The greatest benefit of building a hope chest is this: you will free *yourself* in the process. Every time you open your hope chest, you will have an opportunity to commune with yourself while manifesting your heart's desire. You will know you are free when you no longer worry about matters you cannot control. You will know you are free when you are able to show compassion and express love to everyone you encounter. You will know you are free when you do not feel a need to defend your point of view. You will know you are free when you are able to forgive and surrender the grievances of the past. You will know you are free when you recognize that you are the source of your own happiness. In a world filled with conflicting ideas, unrelenting temptations and questionable influences, there is hope. We all have the power to create the life we desire.

About the Author

ROD TERRY is the author of three books: *Brother's Keeper: Words of Inspiration for African-American Men* (Peter Pauper Press, 1996); *One Million Strong* (Duncan & Duncan, 1996) (Recipient of the 1997 New York Public Library System award for best book); and *Kwanzaa: The Seven Principles* (Peter Pauper Press, 1997). He is also a contributing editor in *Wisdom for the Soul of Black Folk* (Gnosophia Publishing, 2007).

Currently, he is employed by the American Bar Association as Associate Director of the Council on Legal Education Opportunity. He is a graduate of Howard University School of Law, Washington, D. C. and Hendrix College, Conway, Arkansas. He lives in Washington, D.C.

Acknowledgments

MANY SPIRITS have inspired or assisted me in writing this book. I would like to thank Felice Robinson, CeLillianne Green, Adrian King, Tammie Mooreland, Cynthia Carson, Tracy Ellis, Natalie Taylor, Clarence Nero and Laura Zamfir for reading early drafts of the manuscript and giving me their valuable insights and encouragement. I would also like to thank my mother, Eursalean McDonley, who is a constant source of inspiration and strength. Finally, I wish to thank my lifelong friends, Ray Howell and Sandra Collier, for their unwavering support and lasting friendship; and my new friend, Donna Boozer, for her patient and loving spirit.

Other Books by Rod Terry

Brother's Keeper: Words of Inspiration for African American Men

One Million Strong

Kwanzaa: The Seven Principles

Wisdom for the Black Soul (contributing editor)

ORDER ONLINE

To order additional copies of *Hope Chest* visit

www.rodterrybooks.com

To order by mail, send a check or money order for
$19.95 (add $4.00 for shipping and handling;
DC residents add 5.75% for sales tax) to:

Enaas Publishing
18 R Street, NW
Washington, DC 20001
(202) 232-3389